Fair Winds &
Calm Seas

Wm Tom Johnson

"Twenty years from now you will be more disappointed by the things you didn't do than by the ones you did. So throw off those bowlines. Sail away from the safe harbor. Catch the trade winds in your sails. Explore. Dream. Discover."

-Mark Twain-

SAILING THE DREAM

A Dentist, a Belly Dancer & a Talking Parrot

Wm. Tom Johnson, D.D.S.

FIRST EDITION

Information for Nautical Terms: refer to *Chapman Piloting & Seamanship* or www. (Search Engine of Your Choice).

Disclaimer: Any typos can be attributed to *"Demon Rum"*.

Special thanks to Teresa Sayre, St. Croix, Jan Zeller & Cecil Bailey aboard *Patriot* (Hylas 46), Sarah & GB Bucknell aboard *Djarrka* (Noresman 447) and Bonnie Parker, League City, TX for their help & valuable suggestions.

ISBN-13: 978-1461078920

ISBN-10: 146107892X

DEDICATION

To

Millie Johnson

{My Sailmate & Wife}

Without her this most unusual adventure would never have occurred. She saved our beloved sailboat by yelling at me, "Isn't this a sailboat? Let's just sail out of here!" during Hurricane Klaus in 1984. And without hesitation she frantically started hauling up the mizzen. She deserves most of the credit for this amazing experience of a lifetime. I was just along for the fantastic ride!

INTRODUCTION

This book is a true account of an Oklahoma kid born under the sign of *Aquarius* who develops a burning desire to someday see the beautiful clear blue water of the Caribbean. His **Dream** turns into a most unusual adventure with amusing encounters and exciting tales of actual sea stories. The author puts you at the helm trying to save the boat during a horrific hurricane. What happens when a 149-foot island freighter rams the anchored boat in the middle of the night? The decision to fill the forepeak with 14 Middle Eastern dance costumes brings an unusual twist to this cruising story. As an added feature, there is a 40-year review of how the cruising experience over the decades has changed through this author's eyes while living in the islands. Lastly, how this whole experience has changed this couple's lives to become **Island People**.

***** Not your Typical Cruising Story *****

TABLE OF CONENTS

1

THE DREAM

I can remember when the **Dream** started to be etched into my memory. It was a cold winter day in the library at Oklahoma State University when I was 19 years old. I was taking a break from my studies and was rummaging around the magazine section of the library. I had always been involved in water sports ranging from swimming, lifeguarding, water skiing and even skin diving. I just happened to pick up a recent copy of *Yachting Monthly*.

I was shocked by what I saw. There was this beautiful sailboat on the cover that looked like it was floating in air above the seafloor. From that day on, I knew this was an experience that would be in my future. Little did I realize what a major influence the seas would have on my life? I would someday experience that picture on that cover.

The following summer in 1959 about 30 of us OSU students wound up in California working mostly at Disneyland. The pay was $2.45 per hour and it sure beat plowing land on a John Deere for 50 cents per hour in Oklahoma. Besides, I wouldn't be covered in a layer of dirt and sweat since closed air-conditioned cabs had not been invented.

We would spend most of our free time on the beaches around Huntington Beach. I must say that coming from Oklahoma this seemed to be paradise with all the water activities and sights. Plus, there were all those

California women in two-piece bikini suits. This was a completely new experience since the girls in my area of the country had not taken to that fashion statement. You can imagine what effect a vision like that would have on a 19-year-old college boy. Needless to say, 130 OSU students went to Southern California the very next summer.

During those heady summer days, I was able to fulfill one of my longtime desires. Since childhood I had been swimming in ponds, lakes, gravel pits and pools. I was fascinated by the underwater world. Many things sparked my desire to learn more; everything from *Frankie the Frogman* comic books, *Skin Diver* magazine and stories from an ex-UDT employee of my dad's who was in the Inchon Landing of the Korean War. I took the LA County SCUBA course in Long Beach. The course cost $25 and included all the equipment plus an all day trip on their boat to Catalina Island to qualify for an open water certification. The only safety devices back then was to drop your weight belt and the J-valve which would give you 5 minutes of air at 30 feet or 4 breaths at 170 feet.

This course had only been in existence since 1954 and was one of the first in the United States. It was developed because California nearly banned scuba diving from its beaches due to deaths from this relatively new sport. I naturally took to this endeavor which would become a big part of my life.

Al Tillman, one of the co-founders of the program, signed my LA County certification card. As one of the founding fathers of the sport he was heavily involved with the early TV series *Sea Hunt* and *Skin Diver* magazine. There was a need for a national training program by 1960. Tillman also developed and co-founded the NAUI Scuba

Program. Later, he developed the first dive resort destination in the Bahamas called UNESXO.

SCUBA certification cards: Wm. Tom Johnson

After three years at Oklahoma State University and four years at Baylor College of Dentistry, I was ready to fulfill my prearranged commitment to the USAF serving at Maxwell Air Force Base in Alabama. I jumped headlong into SCUBA diving since I finally had the funds. In the summer we would dive Destin, Ft. Walton Beach and Mobile. Wintertime would find us cave diving around

Defuniak and Morrison Springs. The Florida Keys were always on our diving agenda.

In 1967 after the service, I went to Corpus Christi, Texas to start my private practice. This allowed me to be near boats, the ocean and warm weather. By 1969, I had a 17-foot Powercat outboard boat rigged to launch on the beach. We would plan trips to the oil rigs that were eight to ten miles offshore in 60 to 80 feet of water. We would dive these rigs early in the mornings and later fish the anchored shrimp boats while culling their catch. The only problem we had was that in the winter months the water was cold and the visibility poor.

My boys, the speared catch of the day & the Powercat, 1971

(switched from speargun to underwater 35 mm & movie cameras)

By 1972, the deepwater platforms were starting to work their way down the Texas coast from Louisiana. This provided great diving all year. The only problem was that they were 30 to 45 miles offshore which was too far for a 17-foot outboard boat. The only solution was to have a bigger boat.

By December, I had orchestrated a plan to sell my outboard rig, obtain a US Coast Guard License and purchase a 28-foot Bertram Fly Bridge Cruiser. I set the whole thing up in a Subchapter S Corporation as a charter boat enterprise. All this was to help pay for what promised to be an expensive endeavor. I chartered out of Fisherman's Wharf in Port Aransas on the Texas coast near Corpus Christi.

My charter boat business card, 1973

Captain Tom and Millie on the Bertram "La Isla", 1974

By the next spring, I was practicing dentistry and acting as a charter boat captain on the weekends. I also became involved in a project that developed artificial reefs in Texas coastal waters. I read an article in *Skin Diver* magazine about mothballed WWII Liberty Ships being given to the coastal states by the Federal Government for artificial reefs. I was involved in sinking 12 of these ships with the Texas Coastal Marine Council.

Since, I obviously didn't have enough to do, my companion, Millie, convinced me in 1975 to buy a red London double-decker bus for her new business called Millie's Treasure Chest. She wanted to service conventions, birthday parties, civic events and local organizations' functions. I probably had more fun with that endeavor than any other. Just the unbelievable looks on people's faces when they saw this oddity coming down the road at them was worth its weight in gold—almost.

1952 London double-decker bus, 1975

Whenever a British grain ship was in the Corpus Christi Port, we would drive the bus down to the ship to give them a little taste of home. We were always invited aboard to sample their ample supply of English keg beer.

Another time, the attack ship *HMS Intrepid* visited our port on a goodwill stop. We became good friends with the ship's officers by taking them around in the bus and on fishing trips in the Gulf of Mexico on the Bertram. We still have a metal-etched, autographed plaque of the ship that they presented to us.

We had many interesting times on that 1952 bus from bars hiring us for their Halloween parties to driving to a Willie Nelson concert 30 miles away.

One time, a prominent oil man flew his very well to do oil buddies in for a big party at the Corpus Christi Country Club. We picked them up in this goofy bus and drove down Ocean Drive Boulevard followed by a round trip over the high bridge to an open-air hamburger joint down in the commercial port. They were flabbergasted with the excursion to say the least!

The Chamber of Commerce hired us to escort the Convention of Texas Executives. They became quite unruly, and I can't say what some of them did while going over the downtown high bridge. But I can say the cars passing by had their windshield wipers working.

For a Cerebral Palsy Telethon, we picked up the Nashville country music stars at the airport. The mayor had given them a red-carpet welcome.

Corpus Christi's Buccaneer Days found us escorting the Pirate beauty queens around for their photo shoots. We certainly had a lot of fun with that old red double-decker bus.

2

THE DECISION

By the mid '70s, after going through the gas crisis where gasoline went from 35 to 75 cents a gallon, I had lost interest in the charter boat business. I started thinking that a sailboat would fulfill my needs. Sailboats had become much more affordable due to the switch from wood to fiberglass. Also, the concept of living on a sailboat was becoming popular during this time with magazines like *Cruising World* giving instant knowledge to the process of actually doing it.

The Liberty Ship project that I had been working on since 1972 was winding down by 1977. I had used my underwater super 8 movies as lecture material for civic clubs presentations in the early days of the program to drum up support for the project. Four reef sites were planned from Freeport down to Port Isabel. One of the prepared ships sunk prematurely while towing it to the sinking site so Texas wound up having an extra artificial reef site as a bonus.

One of the perks of that project was getting to go diving with Jacques Cousteau and the Houston Underwater Club on a Shell Platform sitting in 170 feet of water 45 miles off Freeport in the Gulf of Mexico. Another perk was that *Southern Living* magazine in 1975 did an article about my involvement in the Texas Liberty Ship Program.

Dr. Tom Johnson surveys the early-morning activity at Fisherman's Wharf in Port Aransas.
Photographs: Crawford

THE TEXANS

Crusader for Artificial Reefs

Dr. Tom Johnson heard the calling of the sea.

And he answered.

Johnson has a dental practice in Corpus Christi. It's a city he first discovered while enrolled for graduate study in Baylor Dental School. It's a city he knew he would one day call home.

The reason was simple.

Corpus Christi is fronted by the Gulf of Mexico, by the wind-blown sands of Padre Island. And Dr. Tom Johnson knew he must live near, and with, the sea.

Since 1959 he had been an avid scuba diver. And most weekends he can be found exploring the water around offshore oil platforms along the Texas coast.

Initially, Johnson was satisfied to chop through the Gulf tides with a small 18-foot outboard boat. But he kept yearning for the challenge of deep water. He kept looking toward the great drilling platforms that lay more than 40 miles out in the Gulf.

In time, Johnson established Isla Enterprises, a charter boat operation on the South Texas coast that caters to the sportsman who is searching for both a fishing and a diving service. Johnson's 28-foot Bertram Cruiser also gave him an opportunity to venture out to depths he had never seen before.

And Johnson began to realize the importance of artificial reefs. He knew that the Texas Parks and Wildlife Department, back in 1957, had created a series of artificial barriers by dumping car bodies into strategic places in the Gulf.

But during the past five years, those automobile skeletons had badly disintegrated, had sunk into the muddy bottom and out of sight. Yet, though flat, the artificial reefs had helped stabilize the floor of the sea and were still productive in attracting great schools of fish.

Johnson says, "Biologists have always told us that deep-water, high-profile structures attract more fish."

And at Port O'Conner rig, he proved it. The drilling platform, lying 45 miles off the coast, rises up 70 feet into the Texas sky.

Johnson points out, "Around the rig you could find big schools of cobia and amberjack all year long. In fact, the amberjack were so thick you had to push them away. In January and February there were even butterfly angelfish and Beau Gregoris, which you wouldn't expect to find here."

He continues, "In 1972, the ship V.A. Fog blew up and sank, leaving only its mast sticking up out of the water. And immediately there began a migration of fish into the area."

Dr. Tom Johnson thus launched a crusade to establish more artificial reefs in the Gulf in an effort to create a year-round fishing industry in Texas.

He read where a bill had been passed by Congress authorizing the coastal states to use old World War II Liberty ships for artificial reefs. It was believed that perhaps as many as 200 of these old vessels were in dry dock around the country. Further investigation, however, revealed that only 35 or 40 remained in the nation's mothball fleets. Salvage companies had purchased the rest.

Johnson realized there was no time to delay. And it concerned him that the And when he arrived at a meeting of the

Driving an English bus, Johnson tours Padre Island promoting area tourism, another of his many interests.

Texas Council on Marine-Related Affairs, he had a petition with 1,000 signatures urging acquisition of Liberty ships. Johnson would later go to the governor with 4,000 signatures.

Proponents of the measure had been told that it would cost $70,000 to prepare the ships for conversion into reefs. But that didn't worry them. As Johnson explained, "Those ships could almost pay for themselves. They were constructed with 3,500 tons of steel.

"Proper salvaging for the state would put 2,500 tons of copper, brass, and scrap iron back into the recycle market. They could salvage everything but the toot in the whistle. Those ships were worth money, as well as a future, for us."

In addition, Senator A. R. Schwartz, who headed the Texas Coastal and Marine Council, pointed out that each reef site would strongly support both sport and commercial fishing in Texas by bringing in $500,000 a year in the fishing trade.

By extending the season for only a couple of months, the state could almost double its annual fish production.

It was a matter Johnson could understand. For his charter boat had made about 70 trips the year before. And 65 of them came during the summer.

Because of Johnson's efforts, and the efforts of those who believed as he did, the State of Texas reconsidered its earlier position and obtained 12 Liberty ships.

Johnson says, "These reefs will provide a hard, exposed surface area for

Johnson championed artificial reefs because he believed it would boost the fishing industry.

barnacles and other sedentary marine forms to attach themselves. And the crannies provide hiding places for small fish, which, in turn, attract those larger fish sought by anglers."

The ships' hulls are now being prepared for sinking off Port Aransas. Port O'Conner, Port Mansfield, and Freeport, their bilges and oil lines scoured to prevent pollution.

And Johnson continues searching the waters with his cruiser for kingfish and marlin and sailfish. He waits for the day, not too far away, when the reefs will bring him more.

Johnson, a Corpus Christi dentist, also operates a charter boat for fishing and diving excursions in the Gulf.

Texas governor had written a letter indicating the state had no desire to participate in the program.

Johnson began knocking on doors.

Southern Living article highlighting my involvement in the Texas Liberty Ship Program, 1975

My marriage in December 1975 was planned to coincide with the actual sinking of the first of three ships off Port Aransas, Texas. I had based my charter boat operation out of Fisherman's Wharf. We planned to hold the wedding and reception on their 105-foot *Scat Cat* aluminum head boat during the actual sinking. I had made its maiden voyage from Louisiana two years before. The Texas Coastal & Marine Council in Port Aransas held a big Liberty Ship party the night before the wedding.

The weather did not cooperate so the sinking was postponed, but the wedding/reception was held in the Lydia Ann Channel in protected waters. My boat captain married us with a Galveston judge making it legal. Two kegs of beer, boiled shrimp and lots of tamales completed a Texas sinking of yours truly into a blissful life of matrimony.

The Texas Coastal and Marine Council's Liberty Ship Project was completed by 1979. At the time it was widely acclaimed to be the most successful and rewarding reef fishery projects in the nation. This was a project that had been denied by the previous Texas Governor and the Texas Parks and Wildlife for being too expensive to complete. The reefing program did not cost the state one penny. The project actually made over $400,000 by the time it was finished. The Texas Coastal and Marine Council decided to use some of those funds to commission a public service film about the project. Millie and I on the Bertram *"La Isla"* were featured in the movie.

The projected revenue from each reef site was put at $500,000 each year by the additional months of use to tourist diving and the fishing industry. In June of 1979, the Council passed a resolution in appreciation of my efforts. The Parks and Wildlife eventually took over the reefing program by adding donated decommissioned oil platforms to the existing sites.

R E S O L U T I O N

WHEREAS, the Liberty Ship Artificial Reef Program of the Texas Coastal and Marine Council has been widely acclaimed as one of the most successful and rewarding reef fishery projects in the nation; and

WHEREAS, the Coastal and Marine Council was made aware of the availability of liberty ships and the high degree of public interest in such a project in January 1973; and

WHEREAS, the public has been continuously informed of the program and the opportunities for recreation through the efforts of Tom Johnson, D.D.S., an interested citizen; and

WHEREAS, that individual has devoted many hours of his personal time and resources to the furtherance of the overall artificial reef program; and

WHEREAS, the Coastal and Marine Council has not formally expressed its appreciation for his efforts in support of the program; now, therefore be it

RESOLVED, that William Tom Johnson, D.D.S., be formally recognized for his public spirited individual efforts and further as a dedicated diver and fervent fisherman; and, be it further

RESOLVED, by the Texas Coastal and Marine Council at its meeting in Port Aransas, Texas, this 15th day of June 1979, that Tom Johnson be presented with this Resolution of the Council as a small token of our appreciation for his efforts and dedication to coastal causes.

A. R. Schwartz, Chairman

Attest: _____
Howard T. Lee, Executive Director

Resolution presented to me by Coastal & Marine Council in appreciation for help with Liberty Ship Project, 1979

In late 1976, we had sold the Bertram and concocted a plan that would get us cruising on a sailboat in eight years. When we took diving vacations to the various islands in the Caribbean during the holidays, we would spend time in the Miami and Tampa areas looking at sailboats for sale. *Cruising World* magazine gave us great insight into the kind of boat we would need.

We gravitated towards the heavy displacement type of William Garden's *Porpoise* that provided comfort and safety. A lot of these boats were being built in Taiwan at the time. We looked at many and found they were showing problems in the decks and cabin because they were built out of plywood covered in fiberglass. But the hulls were bastions of strength since they were properly constructed of heavy fiberglass.

Saddened by this revelation, we finally decided in December 1977 to buy a 37-foot Irwin center cockpit ketch, a typical production boat built in Clearwater, Florida. What was interesting was that the only sailing experience I had was a very limited time of four hours sailing a Sunfish and a Hobie Cat. We did take a dive/sail vacation on the trimaran, *Misti Law,* for a week to see how we faired while living on a boat in the Caribbean. There was a quick learning curve that many of us soon-to-be cruising people would experience.

I had a wonderful time learning how to sail a large vessel around the Corpus Christi waters during the next two years. One can read how to do it a 100 times. But until you really experience it or "Murphy's Law" bites you in the butt, it only then becomes part of ones basic sailing knowledge.

Irwin 37-foot sailboat named "Sea Tooth" and the dinghy "Tooth Ache", 1978

By late 1979, we had discovered that some of the more respected Taiwan builders had corrected their problems of the decks and cabin top construction. We wanted to go back to the more traditional designs so the Irwin 37 was sold in December of 1979. We were back in Florida looking at boats in the 41-foot range.

About this time, another memorable event took place that would have a big impact on our future cruising adventures. I had a patient in my dental practice who was the wife of a professor and the Director of the University of Texas Marine Science Institute at Port Aransas. She was always asking my wife to go to a belly dance exercise class offered by a local Middle Eastern Dance Troup in Corpus Christi. About the third year of this patient nagging her to go, she finally relented just to get her off her back about it.

I will never forget the night that she went to this exercise class. I was home watching *Monday Night Football* with Howard Cosell and Don Meredith providing the entertaining commentary when she rang the doorbell. When I opened the door, she had the widest grin that I had ever seen. She shouted at me in a deafening voice, "I love this belly dancing! And I am learning everything I can as fast as I can!"

From then on she was on a fast track on this quest. Whether it was local classes or attending workshops all over Texas, she was there learning all the facets of the history, music, ethnic costumes and dances of the various different styles of the dance. Egypt, North Africa, Greece, Lebanon, Armenia and Turkey all have different styles, music and costumes.

While I attended a dental symposium in San Francisco, she was able to take a class from the legendary Jamila Salimpour. We also went to see her perform at a theater downtown. She is the mother of the now most prominent Middle Eastern dancer in North America, Shulaila Salimpour, who was featured in the recent *American Belly Dancer* television special.

Millie's goal was to make the semi-professional six girl troop, the *Tirzvah Dancers,* where she was taking classes. This usually takes years and requires attrition before another can be invited to join. Within a year she made the troop by beating another dancer in a two-day tryout. She took the stage name of Serena. Jokingly, I later became the "Keeper of the Bras" of the troop.

Serena's portfolio flyer for dancing, circa 1980

In October of 1980, we bought a CT-42 Mermaid Ketch in Miami which was a traditional William Garden designed sailboat. It had a classic wine glass stern and a long bow pulpit reminiscent of ships of bygone days. We christened her *s/v Serena* in honor of my wife. We left her in Miami to finish outfitting and planned to return in December for a sailing vacation to the Bahamas.

CT-42 Mermaid Ketch Specification

The weather did not cooperate on our return in December. After a few last minute details, we decided to take our new boat down to Marathon Boat Yard in the Florida Keys to store her on the hard. We had decided to wait till spring to sail her across the Gulf of Mexico to her homeport in Corpus Christi, Texas.

In April 1981, Millie and I with two other crew members flew to Miami. We spent three days in Marathon provisioning the boat. We then sailed down to Key West and tied up at the decommissioned Truman Annex Submarine Base. What was interesting at the time about this historic Naval Base was that it was being used to store confiscated Cuban boats from the mass exodus of the Mariel Boat Lift along its seawall.

The crew enjoyed the sights and sounds of old Key West for another three days. We then moved to Dry Tortugas to wait for a weather window to start our trip across the Gulf nine hundred plus miles to Port Aransas. While there we toured Fort Jefferson and snorkeled around the crystal clear waters of the area.

We started out with 20-knot winds on our aft quarter and large following waves. We had to manage the helm by hand because the autopilot malfunctioned. By the second day, we all had sore arms and shoulder muscles form the heavy work which made me think just why in the hell did I get myself into this mess! The next couple of days were relatively calm which gave us the opportunity to skinny dip out in the middle of the Gulf of Mexico in 12,000 feet of crystal clear water. By the fifth day, we were running out of ice, drinking warm beer and craving a cheeseburger. Six and one-half days after leaving Dry Tortugas we pulled into our slip at the Port Aransas City Marina at two o'clock in the morning. We were at the local Whataburger when it opened at nine that day to have our Jimmy Buffett feast. Our next immediate needs were ice and cold beer for a celebration party on the boat --- a perfect ending to a successful crossing.

3

THE PREPARATION

By late 1981, I had become restless looking at the two years remaining on our eight year plan to go cruising. The situation came to a head during a Christmas dinner with the other dentist I shared the office with. He brought up the idea of expanding our office. I said, "Hell No! I am out of here in two years to go cruising." I told him of my plan to sell my practice to which he responded, "How much?" I threw out a figure I thought was reasonable. He was interested in the proposition. So after two months of negotiations with lawyers, the deal was done. The die had been cast and an actual target date was set for September 1982.

We had lots to accomplish in that time; selling the house, two cars and a bunch of stuff we could not put into storage. The next six months was a hectic roller coaster ride of decisions.

One amusing event was that Millie came to me crying saying that she was going to miss her belly dancing and hated to get rid of her outfits. I said, "Darling, No Problem! We are putting all that stuff in the forepeak of the boat and going to have one hell of an adventure on this cruising sabbatical." Also, I told her that our cute talking double yellow headed parrot named "Captain Hook" was going along for the ride.

By mid August, I was getting a bit nervous because the house and two cars had not been sold. I made a decision that we were going come hell or high water. We would rent the house and just park the cars. By some miracle, we managed to sell everything between my September 1st retirement from dentistry and our September 28th sail away date.

On that date, we sailed across the Corpus Christi Bay from Padre Island to the downtown Marina. We spent 4 days tied up to our Bay Yacht Club to say goodbye to all our friends. The most difficult and heart wrenching task of this whole situation was leaving my two teenage sons with their mother (my ex-wife) in Corpus Christi. We had high hopes of sharing our cruising experiences with the boys in the coming years. On the 3rd of October 1982, we untied our dock lines and sailed out into Corpus Christi Bay to start our ***Great Adventure.***

Sailing away from Corpus Christi on October 3, 1982

4

THE GREAT ADVENTURE – YEAR I

Due to sloppy weather, we decided to take the Intracoastal Waterway up the coast. We spent several days motoring up the inside route to Galveston. We anchored for the night just outside the city. Early next morning, we were instructed to tie up to the city marina fuel docks since they were not busy that time of the year. It was a rainy day so we got into our foul weather gear and broke out our Bumble Bee folding bikes that had 2hp engines to use if needed to tour the town. We spent all day seeing the sites of this old historic seaport.

The next morning, when the fuel dock opened, we noticed that the attendant was very cold to us. My wife put Captain Hook out in the cockpit for his morning look around. When the attendant came walking by, a hearty "Hello!" rang out to him. He stood frozen while the parrot went through all his usual song and dance routines. After listening to "Popeye the Sailor Man" and "Macho Man", the guy nearly fell down laughing.

While we were off the boat the day before, everyone in the marina thought we had locked our kids aboard. Captain Hook's usual location was his hanging cage by a porthole. He had the habit of hollering "Hello!", "Let Me Out!", "Help!", "Hook'em Horns!" and so on trying to get attention. The attendant told us they had meetings in the marina office trying to decide whether to call the police, sheriff, fire department, emergency service, welfare department or somebody else to help these locked up kids with abusive parents. Thank goodness all the new child abuse programs had not been invented. Or surely, we would have been arrested and thrown into the brig before the truth was told. A good laugh was had by all and we went on our merry way.

Clear Lake provided a preview of some of the adventures to follow. We had tied up to a diving buddy's private home dock in an exclusive neighborhood. We were there for a few days when he wound up in the hospital from an alcoholic breakdown. All of this was due to his wife suddenly running off with the doctor down the street. I think she had this all planned so we could pick up the pieces. What a hell of a mess we had fallen into!

Later, we moved over to the Lakewood Yacht Club and settled in for awhile. Millie found out that one of the Houston's Middle Eastern Dance Troops was having a graduation for their advanced students to perform their routines for family and guests. This event was being held in the late afternoon at the Sahara Restaurant which was an authentic Middle Eastern establishment catering to its wealthy oil clients staying in the Houston area. They even had a live band with a Lebanese featured dancer.

The dance troop asked Millie, aka Serena, to be their grand feature for this event. Millie with the Corpus Christi *Tirzvah Dance Troop* had performed at many of their weekend workshops in the past. They wanted her to dance accompanied by the house band. She agreed and the die was cast even though it bothered her since she had never performed with a live band.

It is common for these live bands try to trick and embarrass a new dancer who is not from their ethnic background. She asked them to play a certain melody sequence for her routine. Needless to say, as she made her way from the back of the grand dining room all veiled with her zils clattering the rhythm of the song, the band suddenly stopped playing. She stopped with her arms stretched upwards in a graceful pose for what seemed like forever. The band then started again with a completely different song. She carried on even stronger with her zils and moved about the dance floor wondering how she was going to get up onto the elevated stage directly in front of the band. All of a sudden a small step came out of the stage as if by magic. She danced upon the stage as the smiling musicians nodded their heads in approval. Later, the band members told her that she reminded them of a song about a longhaired dancer.

I was sitting in the back of the room with some of her troop members from Corpus Christi who had come up for the event when I felt a finger tap me on the shoulder. It seems that the club manager wanted to talk to her about hiring her to dance at the restaurant.

During the following weeks, she danced at the club for their nightly shows. The in-house Lebanese dancer was a tad ticked off by this American girl wedging in on her territory. She danced several nights for one of King Farouk's daughters which was quite an experience for a Texas Belly Dancer.

The Lebanese dancer had told her not to perform the *Cane Dance* since it was her specialty. During the second week, she did not show up for her first performance so Millie was asked to do it. She quickly changed her outfit and danced the *Cane Dance*. Toward the end of her ditty, the other dancer came through the door much to the chagrin of the club manager. It you snooze you lose!

Lakewood Yacht Club was having a Circus Party complete with an elephant, clowns and a parachutist dropping into the party grounds. They asked Millie to participate. Serena dressed in a gypsy outfit and danced for the crowds which added a bit of spice to the event.

By September 26th, we were going through the Galveston jetties out into the Gulf of Mexico. We had decided to bypass New Orleans and sail around the mouth of the Mississippi to our next port of Pensacola, Florida. One sloppy day, we took a large beam wave that forced water through the butterfly hatch even though we had the hard dinghy tied down over it. Unfortunately, Millie was sitting on a beanbag directly under trying to stay comfortable in the heavy seas.

I was at the helm sitting on our other beanbag drinking a beer, enjoying the ride, when my very wet wife slammed back the hatch to the cockpit and screamed, "I sold everything for this! Do you think this is fun?" I just smiled, "Isn't this great, I feel just like Joshua Slocum" and immediately threw the rest of the beer in my face. She wasn't amused and replied, "This is no fun! I'm out of here when we get to Pensacola." She went back down into the cabin to clean up the mess. By the time we got to Pensacola, the weather was better and I had sweet talked her into staying.

We finally made it into the Pensacola area on the 31st. It was an uneventful passage, but there were lots of oil platforms and seismic boats dragging two-mile long towlines that could have led to a disastrous situation. We really had to keep a sharp lookout all the time on this passage. We were exhausted by time we made a safe harbor.

We took a slip at a marina just inside Fort Pickens for a few days to recoup. Millie danced at the marina for their Friday night party. A group of us even went into

Pensacola to party in the old downtown section of town. We moved later to take a slip behind a dive shop close Trader Jon's and the old Bayfront Auditorium. We really started to enjoy the cruising life and liked the Pensacola area very much.

One little mishap occurred while in Pensacola. I was in need for some oil for the diesel engine. We both got on our trusty Bumble Bee bicycles with the tiny gas engines and headed to a marine store several miles away. Everything went smoothly until we headed back to the boat. Millie was way ahead of me and did not see what happened next.

As I was ridding over some railroad tracks, my front wheel got caught and flipped me headfirst over the handlebars. Just as I hit on my right shoulder, I could see the front wheels of a car pass close by my face. I was able to jump up and continue, but one of the cans of oil stuffed into my nylon windbreaker had broken open. My jacket was completely covered with oil as I returned to the dive shop where we were docked.

They were having a dive club meeting at the store that I had to pass through to get to the boat. They all had a big laugh when this oil covered sailor appeared and got the scoop on what had happened. The total damage report was no broken bones. But I did have a sore shoulder for the next two years.

On November 11th, we sailed past Fort Pickens out into the Gulf of Mexico once again. Our planned destination was Tarpon Springs, Florida. On the 12th, a cold front caught up with us providing our first miserable offshore weather with 15 to 18 foot breaking waves in the early night. It was dark, wet, cold and testing our physical strength. Our old foul weather gear was leaking badly making us very uncomfortable.

I had changed the headsail to the working jib for the storm. Millie was laying on the bagged genoa low in the cockpit in front of the binnacle trying to stay warm. We took a large beam wave that slapped the boat with a thunderous boom. A wall of cold water rushed down the lee deck right on top of her. She just got up and gave me one of those disgusted looks while going down the hatchway. I laughed at her soggy situation trying to put a positive spin on things.

A couple of hours after midnight, I was shivering so badly that I became concerned. I had Millie throw me a nylon sleeping bag that we had onboard. I climbed into it and was able to get some relief from the freezing cold and wet wind. While lying on the cockpit seat, I hand steered using our Combi wind directional instrument to keep the boat close hauled into the wind for a better ride.

By midday, the seas had calmed. We were now back into the groove of sailing to our next port. All of a sudden on the VHF radio, someone was hailing us. We found out that it was a man and his dog fishing for red snapper on what is known as the Middle Grounds in the northeastern Gulf. He had been out there for a week and was wondering where we were headed. When I said Tarpon Springs, he responded that he kept his boat there. We agreed to meet him in two days at Pappas Restaurant where we had planned to dock.

Funny thing was that we never saw him or his boat because of the wave height. We never made the designated date at Pappas due to the cold front. The best we could make was St. Petersburg Beach. We anchored in view of the historical majestic pink Don CeSar Hotel to recoup for the night before moving up to Clearwater.

On November 16th, we took a slip at the city marina. The very next day we went to the nearest marine store and purchased some heavy duty foul weather gear. We planned never again would we be that miserable while trying to stay dry and warm.

We finally made it to Tarpon Springs on the 19th. As we were tying up at Pappas Restaurant, a man walked up to the boat. He said, "Well, I see you finally made it, but you're about four days late." He was the fisherman out on the Middle Ground who we never saw. We had a great night eating Greek food and learning about each other's sea quests.

St. Petersburg was our next big stop that even included the annual Boat Show. On the 3rd of December 1982, we sailed out under the Tampa Bay Bridge and docked that night at the Bradenton Yacht Club. The area smelled like oranges because of all the juice factories. The following morning we toured the town and even got to see "Snooty the Manatee", the local town mascot.

The next day, we motored down the ICW and anchored off the Marina Plaza in downtown Sarasota. We spent three enjoyable days touring the quaint city. We visited the John Ringling's Museum of the Arts which he gave to the State of Florida in 1927. This large complex consisted of his mansion, art museum and a circus museum.

By the 8th, we were anchored in Venice with its charming historic downtown area. We sailed out into the Gulf next to the Pine Islands anchoring overnight behind Useppa Island. Our next stop was Captiva at the beautiful

South Seas Plantation resort for a couple of days. On our wedding anniversary of December 14th, we sailed out into the Gulf of Mexico for Key West.

By December 18th, we had made our way to Key West where we anchored near the old shrimp docks. The place was full of shrimp boats with their hanging nets drying in the sun. An event took place that would provide an interesting project for me during the coming months.

After a late dinner at the Half Shell Raw Bar down by the shrimp docks, we ventured over across the street to an old shrimper's bar. It was a sort of an old local beer joint at that time. The Historic Seaport Village has since changed that entire area into a glitzy tourist destination.

s/v Serena anchored with Captain Tom on the Key West Shrimp Docks, Dec. 1982

As we walked into the place, the old Wurlitzer jukebox was playing a song about Jimmy Buffett doesn't live in Key West anymore. It was very funny and had a catchy tune. Being a big fan of JB, as most sailors are, I went over to the jukebox to see who in the hell was singing this song. I wanted to get it for my collection.

The artist turned out to be none other that David Allan Coe who was famous for his hard luck country songs. I played the flip side of the record and was entertained by an even funnier song titled "Pussy Whipped Again". I immediately knew this was a must-have, but little did I realize the adventures this quest would hold for me.

By the 29th, we had moved on to Marathon. We tied up to the bulkhead next to Sombrero Resort. I made arrangements with the Marathon Marine Yard to pull the masts on my boat so I could strip them of the damaged varnish and have them sprayed with epoxy paint. We spent the next 15 days working on them and getting to know the area.

I found out that David Allan Coe had a home on Big Pine Key, and I was determined to get a copy of those songs. I discovered that it was not in the local record stores anywhere from Key West to Miami. Finally, I realized it was something he did as an underground lark. I found out his whole life had been sort of a big mess.

So on our next trip down to Key West, we found the information we needed from a local dive shop in Big Pine Key. Seemed everyone had a story to tell about him from his big black Hatteras sport fishing yacht with the live Macaw to his over-indulgence.

We drove to his home where I got out of the car and knocked on the door. To my complete astonishment which suddenly turned to delight, this good looking woman opened the door and invited me into the house. I immediately followed since she was only wearing bikini panties and a thin white undershirt that revealed her puppy dog eyes. I did turn and called to my wife to get out of the car and come with me since I did not want to be alone with this woman.

Nonchalantly, she proceeded to tell us that David wasn't there because Willy and Waylon had dragged him off to Nashville to get him cleaned up for the coming awards show. She went on to say that we were probably here to get one of his two underground records or maybe one of the books he wrote while in prison. She had hit the nail on the head, and we proceeded to buy the vinyl LP record.

Looking over to the hot tub in the corner of the room and slyly smiling, she said we were welcome to use it. My wife and I looked at each other and promptly got the hell out of there. Didn't want any trouble in River City!

The next phase of this story is getting the LP converted to a cassette to be able to use it on the boat. I quickly had to use some duct tape to block out the "*MF*" word directly under *Ain't Nothing Sacred* title on the album cover. We were on our way to Key West so I went to a record store to get it converted.

The manager of the store said that he could not make a copy because of the trademark laws and license agreements with the record companies. As I was walking out of the store, I realized that it was an underground production that had none of these restrictions. I explained this to him. He looked over the cover and agreed to make four copies for me.

Several hours later, I went back to the store to collect my valuable treasure. I was met by him with a big grin on his face admitting that he had made several copies for himself. The collection of songs was certainly his motivation because of the X-rated nature. Over the years, I have made many copies for fellow boaters to enjoy.

We spent three months in Marathon removing the masts, booms and stripping the varnish which was in bad shape. We then had the boat yard spray them with 2-part epoxy. We also did trips to Miami, Ft. Lauderdale and of course spent a lot of time traveling through the Keys.

One of our boat neighbors was from South Boston, Virginia which was a rural tobacco growing area close to the North Carolina boarder. He talked us into going up to the Chesapeake that summer before we started our voyage to the Caribbean. The more we thought about the idea; it seemed to be a great plan. We probably never would get the opportunity again. Also, he tempted me by saying that if we visited them in South Boston, he would arrange for us to see the scenic Blue Ridge Mountains by motorcycle. What an interesting and very enticing deal!

Coming from Texas, we did not have any knowledge of the area. I immediately bought a copy of the *Waterway Guide* and found a worn copy of James Michener's *Chesapeake* to start planning the trip. I enjoyed history and the thought of seeing the sites of the old seaports of the founding colonies, the Revolutionary War and the War Between the States would be fascinating.

We started our trek on March 13th, 1983 up the Atlantic Intracoastal Waterway commonly called by boaters The Ditch. We wanted to see all the interesting places and be able to stop and visit certain areas. We motored most of the time, waited for bridges to open and ran aground a lot. But it was fun and exciting to read the *Waterway Guide* for the next day's travel destination. It has mile by mile information complete with aerial photos, sketches, navigation advice and listings of interesting sites.

On the 29th, we were traveling through Jupiter Sound and heard about the coming launch of Challenger 5. So by April 4th, we were in the Banana River with about 200 other boats to view the actual launch at 1:30 in the morning. What a fantastic sight as it lit up the sky with everyone yelling, screaming and sounding their air horns.

In Titusville, Florida we anchored out and rented a car to go to Disneyworld. We also visited the Cape Canaveral area. After traveling four days in a car, we were ready to get moving again. We spent four more days anchored off St. Augustine enjoying this old historic seaport city. We had met many boaters along the way and there were a fair number of them here also. We were like a traveling band of gypsies rummaging around the town seeing the sites

By April 15th, we had weighed anchor and were heading back up the ICW. A day later we anchored off Ft. George Island and toured the old Kingsley Plantation which had a colorful past during the days of the Old South. Strong currents and high tides started to give us quick lessons in controlling the boat as we made our way to Fernandina close to the Georgia border. The entire area had an unpleasant smell from the nearby paper mills.

The 20th found us anchored at Fort Frederica on St. Simons Island where in 1742 the British forces defeated the Spanish ensuring Georgia's future as a British colony. Two days later, we took a slip at Thunderbolt Marina on the Herb River. This was the best place to stop in order to visit Savanna which was too congested for sailboats.

Every morning we would eat the donuts that magically appeared by our hatchway via compliments of the marina and then take the city bus into downtown Savanna. The old historic town was fantastic to explore. We even stood in line to eat the southern fried chicken lunch at the famous Mrs. Wilkes Country Dining Room.

On the 26th, we were in Beaufort. On the 30th, we arrived in Charleston, South Carolina, another major historic seaport town of the Old South. We took a slip in the city marina and spent a few days enjoying the city's rich past. We even went across the bridge to tour the USS Yorktown aircraft carrier.

April 5th, we anchored off Georgetown's historic docks. Our friends on the *s/v Sharon Virginia* were tied on the dock selling their Haitian artworks and tee shirts during the town's Lowland Fling Festival. They suggested to Millie that she go talk to the Chamber of Commerce about having a belly dancer show up for the festivities. Millie gathered up her portfolio and immediately contacted the person in charge.

Of course, they were dumfounded at having a Texas belly dancer on a boat show up at their office. After looking over her portfolio, they realized she was a true professional Middle Eastern dancer and not some exotic performer. They said they would love to have her but couldn't afford to pay her. Her comeback was, "No Problem! But could we tie up next to the *s/v Sharon Virginia* on the city docks for free?" They agreed and also asked if she would be in the big parade the next morning.

The next morning we showed up at the city park at the designated time to be met by a lady from the Chamber. Millie had decided to use her gypsy costume and was covered up in her kaftan robe that she always wore before a performance. The lady did not understand this and ask if that was her outfit. She was relieved to see her costume. We knew there had been some concern about her showing up half naked.

The next fly in the ointment was where she should be in the parade. The policeman immediately suggested for her to be placed directly in front of the police car that would lead the event. Since Millie didn't have any idea of the parade route, she suggested she be placed in front of the Renaissance Troop since a gypsy dancer would fit right into their theme. This was where she ended up only to be constantly dodging the big three-foot high Great Dane dog nipping at her twirling veils and skirts while she clanged her large iron zils.

It was quite a sight as she turned the corner to head down the main street. Even a large crowd of locals sitting on the sidewalk curb jumped up and started shouting, "get down Mama---get down Mama---get down Mama" as they followed her down the street.

Millie, aka Serena, in the Lowland Fling Festival Parade, Georgetown, SC, 1983

The lady at the Chamber quickly arranged for radio interviews and a performance later in the day on the main stage where the bands played. She also insisted that we show up on the way back down from the Chesapeake to be in their fall festival in October.

We also had fun on the dock because a lot of people had seen and heard about this belly dancer from Texas cruising around on a sailboat. So, I quickly made up a sign and placed it on the pin rail advertising about boat tours, a live talking parrot, tee shirts and donations to help support the cruising life to compete with the s/v *Sharon Virginia's* business enterprise.

s/v Serena with "Support the Cruising Life" sign

The rest of the month of May was a flurry of many interesting sights such as Myrtle Beach, Wrightsville Beach, Camp Lejeune and Moorhead City. But Beaufort, North Carolina provided one of my more entertaining encounters.

We had anchored off the city's dinghy docks and enjoyed this town since it catered to all the boats moving up and down The Ditch. The last night we were there a cold front blew in during the middle of the night. I was suddenly awakened by a loud thump on the starboard side of the boat. I jumped out of our berth and rushed to slide the cockpit hatch back to see what had happened.

To my utter shock and amazement, there was a cute and topless French girl practically in my face when I stuck my head out. She was leaning over about a foot away holding off her boat which had dragged anchor. She started explaining what had happened in her sexy French accent of which I did not understand a word. The situation got me so confused that all I could think of was to politely invite her over for breakfast in the morning.

I waited excitedly for her to actually show up but to no avail. This was my first encounter with what the sailors refer to as a *Bare Pair*. The future would hold many of these delightful encounters while cruising in the tropics.

We continued on past Albemarle Sound, Coinjock and to Mile 0 at Norfolk, Virginia where we docked at the city's Kingfisher Docks. That whole area was being revitalized into the Waterside Festival Marketplace and scheduled to have its grand opening in a few days on June 1st, 1983.

All the boats on the dock were cruising people, and they would take turns hosting a party for happy hour. Each of these boats had been cruising long before us and had small guest books. They were filled with personal notes and photos of the people that they had made friends with along the way. Our turn to have the party came on Memorial Day.

As the drinks flowed and everyone got in a jovial mood, they presented us with our very own guest book starting at ICW Mile 0. It was signed by all of the cruisers complete with the notes and photos. It is one of the most cherished treasures of our travels because we can look back at all the wonderful people and memories of our **Great Adventure**. We now have two of these precious books.

Next, we took the boat over to Hampton Roads for a dock slip since we had made plans to visit our boat neighbors in Marathon who talked us into coming to the Chesapeake. We rented a car, packed Captain Hook, a few of Millie's outfits and drove to South Boston.

They had planned a house party to meet their friends and wanted Millie to do her thing. After that party, she was asked to dance at a Rotarian party being held in a few days. Needless to say, the Rotarians of the little town of South Boston had never had a belly dancer show up at one of their functions and were quite enchanted by the event.

Next, we spent three days on motorcycles touring the Blue Ridge Mountains. What a ride! My friend and his wife rode his old classic BMW boxer twin. I was riding a V Twin Yamaha with Millie hanging on for dear life. We were young again ----- like Fonda and Hopper in the movie *Easy Rider.*   * What an experience and a thrill! *

Tom & Millie touring the Blue Ridge Mountains, 1983

After our inland trip, we untied our lines at Hampton Roads and moved on to Willoughby Bay up into the Chesapeake. Deltaville, Virginia was our next stop to pick up mail. Also, I wanted to see where Thomas Covin built his steel and aluminum classic sailing vessels.

We crossed the Big Dirty, slang for the Chesapeake, to Tangiers Island. The place is known for its isolation creating a curious dialect where many of the people are interrelated. There weren't any automobiles on this tiny island. It did have a lot of kids running around on bicycles and ATVs. We were the largest sailboat that had ever been on there tiny town dock, and it created quite a stir. I think some of those teenage boys tried running off with my wife when they found out she was a belly dancer.

We started seeing sea nettles that made swimming out of the question for us. By summer's end, they would grow to large cabbage head jelly fish filling the Bay. The local boaters had these large circular nets they would throw out in the water to avoid the sea nettles --- if they were brave enough to venture into the water.

By late June, we headed 90 miles up the Potomac so we could be in Washington D.C. during its July 4th Festival. We anchored for the night at the halfway mark off George Washington's *Mt. Vernon Estate*. The next day we made it to D.C. and anchored off the Gang Plank Marina.

We were able to use their facilities with their rented key for five dollars. We even could tie up to the dock to fill our fresh water tanks. They even told us that if we gave the key back at the end of our stay, we would get our five spot back. Now, that is what I call a damn good deal!

We spent the next twelve days leaving the boat at nine in the morning walking to L'Enfant Plaza for croissants and coffee. Afterward, we would spend the whole day visiting historical sites and museums. We also rode the subway to Arlington National Cemetery to see the Marine Corps Taps Ceremony at the Iwo Jima Memorial. It is a must-see and a very emotional experience.

On the grassy Mall, two states had pitched tents and booths to show their music, heritage and culture. One was New Jersey which featured their garden and rural communities. The other was Louisiana which was a lot more fun. You could dance to Cajun and Zydeco music and enjoy their spicy food. Late in the afternoon, all the various military bands would give concerts at the different monuments till ten at night.

The 4th of July Celebration complete with fireworks was spectacular. We were back on the boat when the fireworks lit up the sky highlighting the Washington and Lincoln Monuments in a rainbow of ever changing colors. What a fantastic culmination of our country's birthday. They were fun filled days, but we were exhausted by the end of our stay.

We motored back down the Potomac where we decided to stay at *Mt. Vernon* on their dock at their suggestion. The National Park people were amazed that we had traveled by boat all the way from Texas, just as boats did in the past before the age of roads and railways. Our next stop was at the mouth of the Potomac at St. Mary's College for two days to rest. Next, we sailed on to Solomons Island to see the Calvert Marine Museum.

We took a day long sail across the bay to Oxford and anchored for two days. Next, we headed up the Chesapeake to the back side of Knapps Narrows to see the fleet of historic oyster workboats called Skipjacks racing out in the Bay. The following day we passed through Knapps drawbridge to sail on to St. Michaels to tour the Chesapeake Bay Maritime Museum for a couple of days.

We then went out into the bay to clean the bottom of the boat since we noticed there were no sea nettles in the water. After a good scrubbing, we motored across the Bay to Annapolis on a windless summer day.

We anchored off downtown by the Naval Academy. Millie and I spent four days seeing this historic place. We even had the opportunity to see the new Plebes on the parade ground trying their best while about a dozen on crutches and in plaster casts stood on the side.

Next, we spent ten days in Baltimore's Inner Harbor anchored by the Aquarium. McCormick's Old Spice Warehouse, USS Constellation, B&O Railroad Museum, Ft. Mc Henry, Lexington Market, an Italian Festival and a day trip to Gettysburg battlefields kept us running around all hours of the day. The people at the Harbor Place wanted us to tie up along their quay, but we decided not to because the tourists would be bothering us all the time.

By September 8th, we were back in Annapolis. The Naval Academy was having an open house which we enjoyed while touring the campus. During our eight days there, we witnessed one of the most inspiring moments of our Chesapeake adventure. The Plebes were in the stands for their weekly parade day while the Marine Barracks Washington Silent Drill Platoon with their Drum and Bugle Corps performed for the Plebes.

They marched silently out onto the field to a line in front of the young new Plebes and stood at attention. All of a sudden there was a thunderous slap of rifles coming to Present Arms. It so stunned all the Plebes with the precision, they all jumped up screaming, yelling, clapping and shouting their amazement. Millie and I both looked at each other with tears in our eyes from this emotional experience seeing the joy in their young faces.

On July 22nd, we were back in St. Michaels but were tied to their quay in front of the museum. After spending the afternoon enjoying the Maritime Museum, we casually went back towards our boat. Looking around, I saw fellow boaters briskly attending to their boats like something was about to occur. I just happened to look to the northwest only to see the biggest and blackest storm clouds rolling towards us. I remembered reading about these late summer storms.

I immediately made the decision to move out of the small harbor since it was extremely crowded with anchored vessels of all types and sizes. I surely did not want any of them to drag down and damage our boat.

As we got underway, the first wind changes occurred as we went through the harbor jetties into the Bay. In just a few moments the rain and wind made it difficult to see, so I just kept a compass course. I had to put on my dive mask because of the stinging raindrops. Looking at the depth recorder, I went to where I was free of the channel to anchor for the night.

Our third stop in Annapolis was interesting because the Plebes paraded for the Naval Academy's Parents Day. We were sitting in the stands with all the parents. Millie and I were shocked at how smartly they performed. Even the Plebes Drum & Bugle Corps out-performed the Academy's in house band.

We were so fortunate to see the transformation from a scraggly bunch of raw talent to such a professional group. It even became more emotional when a family sitting in front of us screamed with joy when they saw their son. Millie and I both congratulated them and found they were from Puerto Rico which was an island destination in our future.

By August 6th, we were back at the Kingfisher Docks at Norfolk. In two days, we were headed back down the ICW starting at Mile Marker 0. Names of our anchorages rolled past one by one such as Coinjock MM-49, Albemarle Sound, Catfish Point on the Alligator River MM-94, Pamlico Sound, Oriental MM-181 and the Neuse River. Towns slid past such as Wrightsville Beach MM-283, Myrtle Beach MM-337, Isle of Palms MM-458 and on to Hilton Head MM-553.

On August 18th, we finally got a good weather window to go outside into the Atlantic Ocean from Hilton Head, South Carolina. It was a great open water sail down the coast. We went through the Fernandina Beach jetties MM-716 at three in the morning. Halfway through the jetties, we suddenly noticed a long black shape silently gliding past us heading out to sea. It must have been a sub from the Kings Bay Naval Submarine Base.

5

THE GREAT ADVENTURE – YEAR II

By 23rd of August 1983, we were back in St. Augustine for two weeks partying with the cruiser friends we had met along our journey. Next, we stopped at Marineland on September 7th where Captain Hook made friends with their parrots. We took a slip in Daytona for a few days to get fuel and water. We then moved on and anchored at New Smyrna Beach MM-848 in order to see the town.

By October 7th, we were anchored off Titusville where we rented a car to visit Orlando and Epcot Center. Before departing Titusville, we went to our first container store to stock up on food supplies. We bought two cases of canned bacon which surprisingly lasted three years before the few remaining cans began to spoil. We enticed many boaters over those years with the smell of bacon frying in the morning drifting through the anchorages.

By the 14th, we anchored by the Mouth of the Dragon in Melbourne MM-918 for a quick tour of the area. On October 19th, we were back in Ft. Lauderdale MM-1065 where we rented a slip on the west side of Hendricks Isle.

We started provisioning and working on the boat to get it ready for our offshore passage. We installed a wind generator and a $2,400 Magnavox SatNav which was the first satellite navigation instrument for boats. Two heavy duty 8-D batteries replaced our 4-Ds that were dying. I had to run a small 500-watt Honda generator for five minutes before I could start our diesel engine every morning for the past month coming down the Ditch.

On December 1st, we did a day-long haul-out to paint the bottom and change the zincs at Royal Palm Yacht Basin in the Dania Cut. Next, we moved to Maul Lake to anchor for the night followed by a couple of nights on Monty Trainer's dock at Dinner Key. By the 12th, we were anchored in "No Name Harbor" on Key Biscayne ready to cross the Gulf Stream to Cat Cay in the Bahamas.

We had decided to island hop down what is called the Thorny Path to the Caribbean. The alternative was a straight shot out east 600 miles before making a right hand turn to the Virgins approximately 12 to 24 days land to land depending on the weather.

The next morning at five o'clock seven cruising sailboats weighed anchor to cross the Gulf Stream for the Bahamas. We all had a great sail over with twelve knots of wind and waves varying four to eight feet. We were cleared into Cat Cay Customs right before quitting time at four in the afternoon.

The next day most of us crossed the banks to Chub Cay. Our small group of boats spent the next several days enjoying the crystal clear water and hunting for lobsters. After a night at the bottom of the Berry Islands, we had to motor sail to Nassau because of light winds. We obtained approval from harbor control to enter a little after four in the afternoon.

We all had a great time seeing the old town and met many of the boating community anchored in the harbor. The men of our merry band especially enjoyed seeing the football games on the Casino's TVs while the ladies shopped, gambled and gossiped.

Millie and another boater's mate, after having a few drinks, made a game of finding loose change and dollar bills on the Casino's floor. The most profitable areas were around the slot machines. They became quite good at their new found hobby.

Next, we made a three day trip to see the black iguanas at Exuma's Allen and Highborne Cays. While there on December 29th, we ran out of propane for our stove and had to backtrack to Nassau to get our two tanks filled. The other boats continued down the Exuma chain.

We decided to head over to Eluthera instead of trying to catch up with our sailing group. While anchored in Governor's Harbor, I discovered a Club Med on the Atlantic side within walking distance. Needless to say, it sparked my curiosity. So, another boater and I spent the afternoon partaking of the delightful atmosphere and free food. The next day another couple of male sailors who heard of our exploits and treats forced us to show them the way to the Promised Land.

All was going as planned as we sat at a table for the splendid noontime meal complete with a carafe each of red and white wines. We noticed our buddies sitting two tables over were being escorted off the property, much to our amusement.

Since we were dressed like the typical guest, we finished the meal by trying the French pastries. Later, we went over to a table of freshly cooked pizzas. After that, we enjoyed a generous round of various flavors of home made ice cream. I do believe that we were a tad piggish.

Oh! We thought we had gone to heaven. It had been a long time without such delights. The best part was that it was all free! When we got back our boat, our mates told us of the rapid departure from the anchorage of our brethren pirates in crime. Seems, they were bit nervous of the possibility of being arrested and thrown in jail.

We planned to sail west back to the Exumas. So, we moved down the coast and anchored in a marina resort being developed at Cape Eleuthera. The next day we sailed for Conch Cut in the middle of the Exuma chain. About midday, we noticed a strange ten foot bow wave but no boat off our port aft quarter. We finally read in our guide book that this area was used as a speed testing course for submarines by the U.S. Navy. This probably explained why we did not see what was producing this strange phenomenon.

We anchored that night at Conch Cut. The next morning we had a big beach party with other cruisers. One of the highlights of this island is swimming in the grotto which was made famous by the James Bond movie *Thunderball*.

Next, a memorable nighttime party in Cave Cay where Millie stepped off the boat into thin air followed by a big splash. Crystal clear water and a full moon had disorientated her. Everyone had a good laugh while she was being dragged back onto the boat soaking wet.

By January 21st, we were anchored in Georgetown, Great Exuma with approximately 120 other cruising boats. Everyone we met asked us about the story behind the cow chips. Most boaters listen to the VHF radio for news, entertainment and emergencies. All were intrigued when they started hearing one late afternoon that some boats anchored nearby were asking how to make cow chips from paper, water and flour. They did not understand why three boats were in need of cow chips while others had no idea what they were!

The mystery was solved when we explained that we were initiating some Yankees to be honorary Texans. It was all part of our elaborate testing to see if they were any good at tossing them. Also, we timed them running up and down the beach while holding a large Texas Flag. The last test was how well they could imitate a wild Texas Longhorn kicking up dirt while getting ready to charge. They barely passed, but since it was time for a beer, we agreed to bestow upon them the title of Honorary Texans. And that was the end of the great cow chip mystery.

Georgetown has been a popular way station that has attracted boats going up and down the island chain. Also, it is a wintertime destination for what we termed the snowbird fleet. For years the boating communities in the northeast U.S. and Canada would flock to Georgetown to camp out during the cold winter months. By 1999, the number of boats making it their winter playground has more than tripled to over three hundred.

The town has been very friendly and provides lots of amenities for the cruising community. Peace & Plenty Hotel provides mail drops, a weekly freight boat for supplies, and they even had a commercial airport. So many different anchorages provided ample exploring opportunities and boat party functions. The town has a weekly beach BBQ for cruisers which supports community projects. The Out Island Regatta attracts the old island workboats and was started in 1959. The annual Georgetown Cruising Regatta was started in 1980 and is a favorite with the cruising people.

We even had a boater's swap fair to get rid of one's junk or to buy another's discarded item. We sold our very used rusty Bumble Bee bicycles. One of our fellow band misfits had his wife walk around the beach in a white tee shirt emblazoned across the front "Wanted One SatNav." She definitely caught everyone's eye since she was so very well endowed.

A couple we knew from Corpus Christi arrived by plane after getting married in Nassau. Millie decided to throw them a second Pirate Wedding on our boat. To do the deed up properly, 14 couples boarded our boat at the sound of the conch horn. The extra weight caused our boot stripe to completely disappear under the water.

The official function took place with Captain Tom reading the wedding vows from *Chapman's Piloting*, known as the boater's bible. The bride was adorned with a beautiful island pareo and the groom with a tee shirt and white pants. After the deed was done, Captain Tom kissed the bride, jerked off his clothes and dove from the bow pulpit to everyone's astonishment.

Captain Tom & the Pirate Wedding on the bow pulpit, 1983

A beach party ensued with "derbs" and drinks. The newly remarried couple sat under a makeshift cover of palm fronds on their beanbag thrones. The theme was from Herman Wouk's book *Don't Stop the Carnival.*

One of Millie's experiences happened at the popular pizza joint there in Georgetown. Every Friday night, it was sort of a hang out for all of us boaters to get our weekly pizza fix. Some of our friends asked her to dance, to which she replied "No Problem." It proved to be a fun time. The party was held on the second story flat roof made into an open air bar under the stars. She ended the routine dancing while playing her zils and with a sword balanced on her head.

While enjoying the pizza and beer, we noticed that many of the local island children were running around with sticks balanced on their heads. It finally dawned on us they were trying to emulate her sword dance.

Later, everyone started to peel out of the place and walk back to the dinghy dock. Millie was covered up in her kaftan robe, and I was walking along next to her giving her lip service about something. She noticed that two guys from Montreal were directly behind us on one of modern aluminum sailboats. Finally, tired of my ranting, she blurted out, "I'm going to trade you off for two Frenchman." From behind, we heard "Oui, Oui. Mademoiselle" and they immediately volunteered to be the ones! I think they had been mesmerized by her dancing. Anyway, she had just put me in my place and zipped my lip.

By March 20th, I had eaten so many lobsters that I became allergic to them. And we decided to start our journey down island by sailing to Long Island followed by a jump to the uninhabited Conception Island. We then sailed to Rum Cay where we anchored by the town's dive shop for several days to enjoy snorkeling the reefs.

On the 30th, we weighed anchor at 8:45AM for a long overnight sail to Mayaguana. As we got offshore of Rum Cay, the water was so clear you could see the bottom 70 feet down in detail. After traveling through the night, we rounded Mayaguana late in the day. The anchor splashed at the southeastern end just as the sun went down.

At ten in the morning on April Fools Day, 1984, we got underway for the Turks & Caicos. We hauled down the Bahamian courtesy flag. We took the entire day to make Provo and entered the west passage. The next day we checked in and out with Customs. Then, we took off down the west side of the Turks & Caicos bank with another boat south to French Cay where we anchored for the night. Some Haitian Conch fisherman had set up a camp on the island. Both sailboats weighed anchor early in the morning to cross the deeper route over the banks to the east side for Ambergris Cays.

Each boat had to keep a lookout person on the bow to avoid the shallow coral heads. Darkness fell on us just before we reached our goal so we just threw the anchors over board since we could not see. As the sun came up in the east the next morning, we were shocked to see large black coral heads all around our boats. We felt very lucky as we picked our way to deeper water.

Getting offshore, the Turks & Caicos courtesy flag was stowed. And we headed for Hispaniola in the Greater Antilles. We had a great sail for half the day. But we had to motor when the wind suddenly died. We traveled throughout the night and made good easting in our course. About midnight, I started to smell something burning and checked the boat to no avail. Later, we noticed onshore lights of the island and realized the smell was the burning of wood charcoal that was used for cooking. When the moon came up we could make out the island's high mountains in the background.

We were able to make the northeast end of the Dominican Republic in the morning. We checked into Samana just missing the notorious sailing author Tristan Jones in his trimaran. We were anchored there for 16 days while taking trips to Santo Domingo and Puerto Plata.

Millie danced at a newly opened casino hotel across the anchorage in Samana. An Italian film crew was staying there while making the epic mini-series about Christopher Columbus that was nominated for two Emmys in 1985. They were quite impressed with her dancing and invited us out to their film set on the north shore.

On April 24th, we headed out into the Mona Passage to Puerto Rico. It was commonly referred to as the Moan & Groan Passage by sailors because of the large Atlantic swells and confused seas. The sailboat following us would completely disappear sometimes behind an enormous swell. Millie, on midnight helm duty, woke me on seeing a mass of lights off to our port. It finally dawned on us that it was a cruise ship heading towards the west. Thirty hours after our start, we arrived in Boquerón, Puerto Rico and anchored in its picturesque bay.

We spent twelve days enjoying the small village and even took a side trip via a taxi called a Por Puesto to Old San Juan. Our plans of sailing the south side of the island changed when we found out there was going to be a gathering of Tall Ships in San Juan. We sailed back out into the Mona Passage around the northwestern tip of Puerto Rico heading east for some twenty hours.

We sailed past the old majestic fort of El Morro and anchored by the San Juan Yacht Club right in the heart of the Condado. After a few days of R&R, we just happened to stop by the Tourist Bureau in Old San Juan. We explained that my wife used to work in the hotel/tourist industry and that we lived on a sailboat. They promptly gave us a complete participant packet for the coming Tall Ship Festival.

Now this packet included many free folkloric shows at the various hotels, tickets for all the parties and exclusive tickets to board the Tall Ships. Our days and nights suddenly became a whirlwind of events culminating at the grand sail away party for the participants at the famous Plaza De La Marina.

While touring Old San Juan, we just happened to walk by a large dumpster to throw our paper cups away. Most cruisers become "dumpster divers" over the years since they constantly dump their own trash. I just happened to spot a discarded mannequin leg. I immediately pulled it out, but Mille objected to my new found treasure. I relinquished and threw it back in the bin.

We stopped at a grocery store a block away. While Millie was busy shopping for some supplies, I could not resist the temptation of having that leg. A few minutes later as my mate was checking out, I boldly walked up to the cashier and ask if he had a large bag that would fit this leg. They were both stunned by the sight of the leg. It turned out that I had to use two smaller bags to get the damn thing covered. Even on the bus ride back to the boat, the damn leg kept popping out causing a lot of stares and laughs.

During our month long stay in San Juan, I was able to upgrade my U.S. Coast Guard License to a 100-Ton ticket and pass my Technician ham license. We realized it was time to move on to the east. The only problem was when we hauled the anchor. I had to use a steel wire brush while Millie poured buckets of water to clean the debris that had grown on the chain. This proved to be the longest and messiest anchor haul of our boating years.

Our next destination was Culebra with all of its many anchorages. Two sailboats that we had met in Florida and the Bahamas sailed into our secluded spot. I immediately put the female mannequin leg I had found in Puerto Rico into our dinghy hanging in the davits. I placed it in such a compromising position sticking out of the dinghy that it wasn't long before I got my hilarious response.

Both males in their respective boats had their binoculars trying to see what kind of unusual sexual acts were happening aboard our boat. In about ten minutes, they couldn't stand it any longer and called on the VHF radio. I had the last laugh explaining about the leg. I had many such amusing adventures with that goofy leg. Sometimes, I would stick it out a porthole just as a boat would pass by to see the response. Millie finally made me throw it overboard a few years later.

On June 6th, the Seven Seas Cruising Association, an organization of cruising people, had a party in Culebra. The organizer of the party was a cruiser who had settled there and started a business. He was also involved in the Caribbean Maritime Net on the ham radio so the word got out and we had a large turnout of boaters. The SSCA event was a roaring success.

By the 18th, it was time to go to the U.S. Virgin Islands so we weighed anchor and sailed on east. After getting fuel and water in St. Thomas, we moved on to Christmas Cove and anchored for a couple of days. We then moved on to St. John to anchor by the famous Rockefeller Resort of Caneel Bay for three days. We would dinghy into the town of Little Cruz Bay to enjoy the sights and sounds.

After a short trip to the British Virgin Islands, we were back in St. John for the big Fourth of July celebration, complete with a parade and fireworks. From there, it was back and forth between the USVI and the BVI until we did an open water sail to St. Croix forty miles away to the south.

We spent ten days on St. Croix enjoying the historic town of Christiansted and Buck Island. The Kennedy Administration had an enormous impact on St. Croix. John F. Kennedy established the Buck Island National Monument in 1961. These years are often referred to *The Camelot Years of St. Croix.*

Several of his administration people retired on the island. They brought others such as the actress Maureen O'Hara and her husband Charles Blair, a pioneer in transatlantic aviation. In fact, he started the first seaplane shuttle here on St. Croix that lasted until Hurricane Hugo in 1989. Many famous and important people have bought property and lived on the island throughout the years.

On Labor Day weekend, we were at Foxys Wooden Boat Festival on Jost Van Dyke in the BVI. It was quite a party with all the drunken sailors and many *Bare Pairs* to view. The harbor was jammed to the gills with sailboats overflowing into the adjacent anchorages. Nighttime became a bumper pool boat mania, but no one gave a damn since it was *Party Hearty Mates.* By early dawn, it was comical to find out who was on whose boat.

Another thing which happened in the Virgins was that we became an interesting item for many of the charter boat sailors. They would slowly dinghy around our classic sailboat with a look of curiosity often asking questions about cruising and our sailboat. Many of the bareboat charters would offer us their remaining provisions as they returned their vessel back to the charter company.

Also, it was amusing to see the charterers acting out their dreams of being pirates, dressing wildly and being unruly. The participants of the "au natural" group were always interesting to watch, especially with a good set of binoculars.

We were really getting to know the Virgin Islands and enjoyed them to there fullest. In sloppy weather, we would sail to our destinations in Sir Frances Drake Channel to avoid the large swells. In calmer weather, we would venture out into the open sea to experience its vastness and beauty. We became familiar with the quaint ports such as Spanish Town, Road Town, Great Harbour, Charlotte Amalie, Christiansted, Little Cruz Bay and the list goes on. Names on the charts started to become actual places that one could visualize bringing a smile and a new sea story to tell.

The names of the most beautiful beaches became actual sites to see and enjoy. Cane Bay, Rainbow Beach, Buck Island, Hawksnest, Maho, Cinnamon, White Bay and the Baths brought a sense grandeur that one had to experience to fully appreciate.

The newspaper *Caribbean Boating,* distributed from New England and throughout the islands, published an article about us in July 1984. It was the only boating newspaper at the time and widely read. At the time, St. Thomas was the charter boat capital of the Caribbean. We certainly did not fit the typical sailboat cruiser. We started to even get more attention after it came out.

Cruising Aboard "Serena" In Company With A Bellydancer, A Diver/Dentist And A Talking Bird

QUESTION: What do a belly dancer, a dentist who has dived with Jacques Cousteau, and a parrot with a penchant for dark-haired women have in common?

ANSWER: All three are cruising the Caribbean aboard the 42-foot CT Mermaid ketch "Serena."

Millie and Tom Johnson, accompanied by their three-year-old Amazon parrot Capt. Hook, left Corpus Christi, Texas, two years ago to pursue the cruising life. Since then they have travelled to Florida, up the U.S. East Coast to the Chesapeake Bay and through the Bahamas and Greater Antilles before arriving in this part of the world a few months ago.

And, should the need arise as it does at one time or another for most cruising folks, Millie has an interesting way of replenishing the cruising kitty. She merely goes up to the forepeak, selects one of her 15 costumes, dusts off her sword and drums and is ready to perform. She's danced in clubs, festivals, and for private parties all along their route.

Millie originally became interested in belly dancing through a patient of her dentist husband but says she was very skeptical at first.

"I had the wrong ideas about it and didn't know what other people would think," she explains. After one lesson she was completely hooked, and within a year, earned a position with a dance troupe, taking "Serena" as her stage name.

Tom, while appreciative of Millie's dancing skills, is more into diving. From 1972 - 76, he was instrumental in the sinking of 12 liberty ships off Padre Island, Texas to form an artificial reef on the otherwise barren, sandy ocean floor in that area. As a result of his work on this project, he did a dive with Jacques Costeau to view the outcome.

Likewise, Tom also brought the tools of his trade along with him. He can run his dental instruments off a SCUBA tank or his HOKA compressor and is assisted by Millie. Although he isn't practicing dentistry afloat, Tom says "if a sailor in an isolated anchorage has problems, I could help him out."

The final member of "Serena's" crew, Capt. Hook, has a 25-word vocabulary, including phrases of "Macho Man," "Popeye the Sailorman" and, being a true native Texan, "Hook 'Em Horns." His infatuation with dark haired women probably stems from infancy when dark-haired Millie hand-fed him warmed baby food and mashed seeds.

After a four-year jaunt through the Caribbean, if the cruising life still appeals, the South Pacific may be seeing some of the bellydancer, the dentist and the bird.

-B.C.

Millie and Tom Johnson with Capt. Hood aboard their yacht "Serena". (Barbara Camera photo)

"Caribbean Boating" article while in St, Thomas, July 1984

6

THE GREAT ADVENTURE – YEAR III

We had a busy summer, but it was coming to an end. After spending some quality time at the Bitter End Yacht Club where boaters gather for a weather window to cross the Anegada Passage to St. Maarten, our thoughts turned to heading east to the next group of islands. We left North sound on Virgin Gorda, BVI in the late afternoon and went around Necker Island for our overnight sail. The sail was uneventful. As the dawn emerged, we were in the cockpit listening to the song "Island" by Jimmy Buffett. Suddenly, St. Maarten started to appear through the grey haze just as JB sang those same exact words.

We both ran up to stand on the bow pulpit to see if we were imagining. We looked at each other during those magical moments to find each had tears streaming down our cheeks. It is a powerful song for those who have sailed at night and have experienced the same phenomena.

We decided to sail into Marigot, St. Martin since it was a straight rhumb line into the harbor. After checking in to the French Customs, we lowered our yellow Q flag and raised the French courtesy one. Marigot is a wonderful town with its modern French flair and old island charm. It has a large anchorage with good holding for boats to anchor.

The male members of our cruiser group soon started volunteering to go to shore to buy a bag of fresh croissants for our sleepy mates. We would always spend a little time sitting down on the curb to sample the hot croissants and a fresh cup of coffee.

The truth of our devious plan was to watch the sexy French girls in their loose fitting shorts, revealing blouses and semi-heels with fluffy little socks going to work. All I can say is that it was time well spent.

Next, we spent five days in Orient Bay on the northeast coast of the island. It was interesting because of the nude resort. We had become accustomed to this European idea since being in the tropics. Most cruisers had accepted the basic rule: *If you don't wear it – You don't have to wash it!*

Since fresh water costs money, you can use that investment to buy boat drinks. It was a simple concept for simple people. All one needed was a French wrap called a pareo. It could be used as a swimsuit, a cover up, a sarong, a shirt, a dress, a pair of pants, a tablecloth, or a sunshade all in the same day.

One of our amusing cruising moments happened when we were at the resort's restaurant eating cheeseburgers. A completely nude couple walked up to our table and said, "Are you off the *s/v Serena?*" Millie nearly chocked on her hamburger because the guy was standing right in front of her and she was at eye level with his *Ting.* I told him that we were and introduced ourselves.

Well, they proceeded to tell us they had just been aboard our sailboat and explained what had happened. They had met one of our boating friends headed back up island in the Bahamas, and they suggested to say hello if our paths crossed.

Seems they had come up to our boat by dinghy and said, "Hello." They were greeted by a loud "Hello" followed by, "Come Aboard." They climbed aboard and sat in the cockpit waiting for us to slide back the hatch and come out. After sitting for several minutes, they remembered we had a talking parrot. Seeing that the latch was locked, they finally figured out it was our notorious Captain Hook who had invited them aboard. We all had a good laugh, and Millie was able to finish her meal.

Another event at Club Orient occurred when we were invited by the owner to come for the weekly Wine & Cheese Party for the new guests. Millie spent the whole afternoon trying to decide what "not" to wear. Finally, she decided on a white University of Texas nylon mesh football jersey that had a large burnt orange head of a longhorn complemented by a white thong bikini bottom. It turned out that she was a tad overdressed.

The new guest party at their restaurant was also very entertaining. The hotel clients in their pareos and various costumes were dancing to the live local band. Throughout the night, the guests became less inhibited and slowly started losing more and more of their outfits. One couple that came as Adam & Eve, wearing only paper fig leaves, didn't have much to lose anyway. By the last song, everyone was dancing as the sailors would call *bare-ass-naked*.

A funny experience happened one day while visiting Club Orient. Another fellow cruiser and I were sunning on the resort's float while our wives were busy visiting their boutique. It seems our boat mates got miffed when they saw the beautiful tall French beach waitress laying between us while we were soaking up the rays. Maybe, it was the fact that we were all nude. I did not have the time to question their reasons.

Both lasses made a beeline for the dinghy anchored beyond the surf line. I told my buddy we better get our butts in gear because we just might be left stranded on the beach. We got back to the dinghy just in the nick of time to prevent a group of young Navy boys from helping them free the anchor.

When Millie had trouble pulling the anchor while standing in the dinghy, she just happened to look back at the beach to see the U.S. Navy boys' eyes trained on her. Trying to push the dagger deeper for our misdeeds, Millie shouted out to them, "Would you boys like to see our boat?"

Every one of them jumped up ready to hit the water because our ladies were only wearing bikini thong bottoms. Those poor boys looked so dejected when we suddenly appeared to ruin their rescue.

There is on old seaman's fable that goes:

"Hurricane in November is Long Remembered"

A trip to St. Barts in November was cut short when an exhaust leak on the boat suddenly appeared. We turned back to St. Maarten where we anchored in Philipsburg harbor to get parts for me to fix the problem. After cleaning up the mess, we proceeded to haul the anchor and get on our way. We then discovered the engine's throttle cable was broken and had to be repaired.

I went back to the marine store for the part which meant we were stuck in the harbor for another day. A tropical depression had formed south of Puerto Rico 250 miles to the west. No one paid much attention to it.

To make a long story short, in two days it was blowing 60 knots directly into the harbor, and we were stuck in a notoriously bad anchorage. Mike Burk's tall windjammer the *Yankee Clipper* was already aground on the middle sand bar. Their West Indies crew had taken the life boats to shore leaving the captain and the paying guests to fend for themselves.

Later, that night Mike Burk's headquarters in Miami told the captain by SSB radio to put life vests on the passengers and let them drift to shore which occurred around midnight. By this time, 34 other types of vessels were washed ashore on the pristine beach of the town.

At 2:40AM with 12 to 18 foot waves pounding our boat, both of our anchor lines parted with a loud bang. We had been running the engine earlier in forward gear to lessen the strain, but we had to shut it down since it had overheated.

As the boat started to drift backwards, I told Millie to go to the helm and try to start the engine. I ran forward to the bow to point to the northeastern side of the harbor to try to get some protection from the wind and waves. Halfway over the engine overheated again and seized up.

As we drifted back, I noticed the *Yankee Clipper* had drifted onto the beach somewhat behind us. We had only the dinghy anchor to use to keep our bow into the waves. As we slowly approached her, I put out on the VHF radio that we were about to be the next vessel to be washed ashore.

I told my mate to go down, pack our valuables, some clothes, put Captain Hook the parrot in our small ice chest with the lid secured and be ready to abandon the boat. She went down but suddenly came out of the hatch and screamed, "Isn't this a sailboat? Let's sail out of here." I looked at her and said, "Are you sure about this?" She was the typical sailor's wife that had put up with her mate's dream of going to sea and was not nautically proficient.

She did not hesitate one moment and started raising the mizzen sail. I ran forward and started hauling up the bagged working jib. It started to flog violently as I finally got it raised. I ran back to the cockpit to finish raising the mizzen. I then told her to take the helm while I worked the winch to tighten the jib.

As the wind caught our sails the boat heeled over and started moving forward towards the tourist catamaran *Maho* that was anchored nearby. Millie put the helm hard over to tack, but it didn't respond. A person on the *Maho* started jumping up and down waving frantically as we headed towards her. At the last moment, I told Millie to try to start the engine so we could force the boat to come about. Luckily, it cranked over and started. We then were able to complete the tack. The boat started to gain way so I killed the engine.

I was luffing the jib 60% of the time just to ease the strain because the forestay was bending too much. There was now a set of 20-foot waves breaking on the middle sand bar, and we were slowly approaching them. I told Millie to put on a life vest, go below, secure the hatch and check the engine water.

I will never forget what happened next. Standing behind the wheel in the cockpit, the boat rose up 45 degrees into the breaking wave coming over the bow. In three seconds, I was standing in waist deep water rushing past me over the tariff rail. I tried to grab cushions, jerry jugs and anything I could that floated past me. The boat shook violently as she pushed through the wave to the other side. She slowed, gained her footing and finally starting to move past the break line.

To this day, I attribute this to the power of the sails. I know if I had tried that with just the engine the boat would have broached and rolled losing everything. Millie told me when she was topping the freshwater coolant tank on the engine that the stream of water was flowing strangely out the container to the intake hole. Luckily, we had made it out the harbor --- so now what?

The 20-foot waves became further apart as we got offshore to make the ride more bearable. I had my wife put out on the radio that we had just sailed out of the harbor. This was for general safety information just in case we didn't show up later. Suddenly, one of our cruising friends who was anchored in Marigot answered back asking what in the hell were we doing out there? Millie explained what had happened while crying most of the time but happy to know someone knew the situation.

Our Zodiac inflatable painter line had become wrapped around the prop shaft the last time we had the engine running. Every time we would go over a wave our inflatable would slap hard against the fiberglass dinghy hanging in the davits. Bang, bang, bang went the night as we rode over those monstrous swells.

When the sun came up in the morning, we decided to alter our course and head around the south shore to the east side lee of the island for calmer seas. There I was able to clear the painter line from the shaft by free diving with a serrated knife. While I was in the water, Millie cleaned the engine sea strainer that was clogged with seaweed.

We motored around to the north side to Marigot just in time to pick up some anchors and rode from our cruising friends. The French had just declared that the harbor had to be evacuated. Hurricane Klaus winds were now clocking around to make that harbor unsafe.

Our little band of boats motored to the safety of Simpson Bay Lagoon on the west side of the island. By the time we anchored in the lagoon the sun was going down. All of us were exhausted from the ordeal. Our sailboat had just traveled completely around the island minus about four miles.

The next couple of days I spent retrieving all my chain, lines and anchors by dragging a small grappling hook behind my dinghy. I discovered why Philipsburg has such a poor reputation for anchoring in bad weather.

While trying to retrieve my buried anchors with scuba gear, I discovered that the harbor has only one foot of loose sandy shale. Under that layer is a slippery gooey mud that an anchor will just slide through if it works down to that depth in stormy weather

A week later we ran into the owner of the catamaran *Maho* in Chesterfields, a local sailor's bar. He told us that he was screaming, "Go for it! Go for it!" as we came close by his boat on that fateful night. Also, he told us that he could see the entire bottom of our 29,500 pound sailboat as it crashed though the huge waves.

I did have to replace all my standing rigging due to the stresses and stains. Later, I wrote a narrative of our ordeal which was published in the Seven Seas Cruising Association's monthly Commodores Bulletin.

We spent a lot of time in Simpson Bay Lagoon after the storm. We met Dudley Pope, a well known British nautical writer, who lived on his 54-foot sailboat. He was a protégé of C.S. Forester, the creator of the famed Horatio Hornblower novels. It was this connection that inspired him to write a similar 18 book series of nautical fiction about Lord Ramage taking place in the 18th and early 19th centuries.

I became addicted to these novels because it really explained the nuances of sailing ships of that era. It was entertaining, to say the least, to read about those early days while swinging gently in my hammock rigged up in the cockpit of my sailboat.

By now, all our cruising friends had been in the islands long enough to fully adapt to the good life. While we were in Simpson Bay, the wife of one of our sailing friends had a birthday party on their boat. It turned out to be a most unusual celebration in that all the ladies showed up topless. I don't know if it was a conspiracy by them, but it sure was the hit of the party. I'm not going to say which was better---the cake or all those *Bare Pairs*!

We had made plans to sail back to St. Thomas in December to welcome a couple that finally sailed to the Virgins. Another cruising couple came with us to fly back to the states from St. Thomas. As we entered the Charlotte Amalie harbor, a large cruise ship was coming out. Our boat wenches were in their typical sailing attire of bathing suit bottoms and no top.

Being the devious captain of the vessel, I ordered everyone to form up on the port side in order to wave at the passengers on the approaching cruise ship. I swear on Blackbeard's grave that the cruise ship listed to port as all the passengers ran to that side to take pictures.

Later, as we anchored by our friend's boat, they were appalled at the improper attire of our mates. As irony would have it, that same couple made a small fortune selling string bikini thongs bottoms in a matching bag in St. Martin. They did this for two seasons sitting under an umbrella on Orient Beach. This sailor of many talents produced the tiny garments at night while his extremely well endowed wife modeled them topless on the beach while he stuffed the cash in his old tackle box.

We spent two weeks in the Virgins showing the couple many of our favorite hangouts and anchorages. Millie danced for the SSCA's Xmas party in Moho Bay, St. John. By December 18th, we were waiting for a weather window back at the Bitter End Yacht Club in order to cross the Anegada Passage to St. Martin. Two days later we did the crossing in 18 hours using the iron genny, motoring, because of little wind. The other sailboat took 36 hours until he finally gave up on only using the sails off of Saba.

As we were resting from our crossing anchored in Marigot, all boats were ordered into Simpson Lagoon on December 22nd due to Hurricane Lily. It was a freaky storm bearing down from the northeast towards St. Martin. The hurricane changed direction at the last minute on the 24th to circle back out into the Atlantic.

A very thankful 1984 Christmas Eve Hurricane party was held at Frick's Watersports for the Simpson Bay boaters. Millie did a Sultan dance for a birthday boy that added a twist to the function. Everyone probably finally got a good night's sleep after dodging all the hurricanes.

A New Year's Eve Party was held on our boat for our friends. We were a little pissed though that due to bad weather we could not sail to St. Barts to hear Jimmy Buffett playing solo at Le Select Bar that night.

We replaced the standing rigging on our boat in early January. After that job was completed, we sailed over to St. Barts to try to catch JB at his notorious bar named

Autour Du Rocher. He sings about the entire goings on there on his *Far Side of the World* album released in 2005. I still remember seeing the string of car lights snaking their way up to the place as Jimmy so describes in his song.

In fact, most of Jimmy Buffett's songs center on his life experiences. And in the crazy '80s, this was so true in the albums of *Hot Water, Riddles in the Sand* and *Last Mango.* Jimmy was living these songs!

We finally did have our cruiser party at Le Select in Gustavia on January 13th 1985. Also, another popular thing to do at this interesting port was to go to Shell Beach near the town around midday and view the sights. The working French girls "a la no top" would go there to improve their tans during siesta time.

After exhausting ourselves in the delights of St. Barts, our small band of sailing rouges had a nice sail to Pinel Island. This was our favorite anchorage on the east side of St. Martin. We spent many days there and even had a gigantic BBQ with a bonfire. The day-charter boats would bring requested supplies back to us from Philipsburg.

By January 25th, our group had moved back to the lagoon where we had parties on Snoopy Island which was a dredged sand bar inside the entrance to the bridge. Millie and I flew to the friendly island of Saba spending a couple of days. After that trip, it was another round of anchorages for a month. Our gypsy band then sailed back to St. Barts on February 21st.

We anchored off Gustavia, and we discovered nearby a black hull sister ship, a CT-42 Mermaid, from Germany named *Meermaid.* We toured each other's boats to exchange ideas and information. We did have a slight language problem. But we all laughed when their "dirty fish" turned out to be "dried fish" and their teak whitener "ayack" was really "Ajax." I'm sure they had the same problem with our southwestern accent.

I bought so many cases of Heineken beer for about $3.50 each because the exchange rate was ten to one on the French franc. This proved to be a problem later on because I started sweating its peculiar smell. I eventually could not stand the taste of their famous brew with its distinctive smelly flavor.

On March 11th under a full moon, we weighed anchor and headed towards St. Kitts. Lush green mountains, fields of tall sugar cane and the magnificent Fort Brimstone greeted us by midmorning. Two other boats sailed with us. Customs and the boat boys gave us a hassle. We just smiled and our good manners got us through the situation. We obtained permission to anchor in Major's Bay for several days. We then moved on to Nevis. Our three boats anchored for three days off the majestic secluded palm lined beach north of Charlestown. It was then a sail to the northwest side of Montserrat for an overnight stay.

The next plan for our three-boat caravan was to sail to the butterfly shaped island of Guadeloupe. All was going well under a brisk wind when suddenly there was a loud boom followed by the wild flapping of my torn genoa. Evaluating the situation, I made the decision to head for Antigua to get it repaired. The other two vessels continued to Guadeloupe.

Later that day, the boat started shaking and rumbling. I quickly jumped down the hatchway to examine the bilge for leaks or some type of engine failure. I found nothing and the noise had stopped. I thought maybe the boat had hit something. When I checked into Antigua Customs, I learned there had been an underwater earthquake. This event evidently had caused the problem. We met up with the two other boats several months later in Martinique, and they had experienced the same situation.

Antigua turned out to be a great decision. We anchored in the historic English Harbour. The place had been the major naval base for 300 years guarding the northeastern Caribbean for the British Crown. The area had been restored becoming a treasure trove of buildings and artifacts named Nelson's Dockyard National Park. The famed Horatio Nelson had served there in his early years.

It was lots of fun walking over to Falmouth Harbor and going to all the various establishments. We enjoyed the weekly Shirley Heights BBQ with the Halcyon Steel Pan band, dancing and watching the majestic sunsets. The area had everything for boating, dining and entertainment. On the quay, the wash lady Mrs. Baltimore would pick up our dirty duds with a call on the VHF radio and return them several days later clean and folded.

We met many more cruisers while anchored in English Harbour. A bunch of us would catch the local taxi bus into St. Johns which was the main town for shopping. One such couple was on a sailboat from Tampa. What was interesting was that the captain was a middle-aged balding man of many hats and caps. He had formed the Dock Foxes International the year before while in Jamaica at a marina. It was a loosely organized group of boaters who enjoyed the good life. His teenage son and an attractive young lady accompanied the man. He had hired her to tutor his son while they took this year long cruise.

View from Shirley Heights looking down at English Harbour

While we were in the cramped bus going to town, the girl explained to Millie how she had replied to a newspaper advertisement for the job. We noticed that the captain and the tutor were "hooked up", so to speak. Millie finally popped the "64 Thousand Dollar" question. With a big grin, she replied that it took only one night for the deed to be done.

We all broke out laughing while bumping along the road to the town. She also told us she was in a bit of a dilemma since her boyfriend from Tampa was expected to arrive in a few days. We thought this should be an interesting situation. Oh well, good island rum will solve just about any immediate problem ---- for awhile!

While looking around Falmouth Harbor one day we stopped by the Antigua Yacht Club. During our conversation with the club's manager about our travels he found out about Millie's dancing. At his request Millie brought her portfolio the next day. The manager was impressed and hired her to dance for the coming Friday and Saturday night dinner.

Antigua Yacht Club
Serena performed at the Antigua Yacht Club, 1985

The word spread quickly and the place was packed for this unusual event. As she came out with her zils clattering to the Middle Eastern music and veiled with only her eyes showing, business as usual stopped. The cooks ran out from the kitchen and waitresses climbed on chairs to obtain a better view from the rear of the room. Guests were jumping up everywhere in order to get a better view. It was a roaring success and the talk of the island. The manager hired her to perform for the next four weeks before the start of Antigua Race Week.

This led to the committee for Race Week to ask her to surprise Don Street, the famous cruising guide guru, at the fun "Lay Day" festivities. She agreed and quickly enlisted the help of two other female cruisers for the event. She gave them a crash course in a few basic steps, movements and dressed them up as harem girls.

Serena dancing for Don Street during Antigua Sailing Week, 1985

Don Street was so shocked that he had trouble drinking his Heineken beer and could barely control himself. The whole episode was even put in the official "1985 Antigua Sailing Week" video tape. As Race Week ended with the last night's Trophy Ball, it seemed by the next day ninety percent of the boats were gone. Antigua had again become a sleepy Caribbean island.

On May 12th, several of us sailed for the island of Guadeloupe with its tall mountains. We all made it safely to Deshaies except for a 32-foot Westsail which was dismasted by the blustery conditions. A side trip by bus to the capital of Point-a-Pitre was fun. The boating guide was correct about the local ladies of the city. They were some of the most beautiful women of the Caribbean.

As we sailed down the length of Basse Terre, we decided to go on to the Les Saints for a better anchorage. In 1782, the British Admiral Rodney defeated the French fleet during the famous Battle of the Saintes by employing a new naval tactic known as "Crossing the T" rather than fighting in parallel lines blasting away at each other ships.

We became friends with the owners of the Mahogany Shop in Terre De Haut while anchored there. The French artist operated a boutique, selling batik clothing and paintings. He was married to an American girl at the time. She befriended any U.S. vessel just for the stateside companionship. Millie and I enjoyed this island for a week.

On May 25th, we hoisted the anchor and motor-sailed north into the center of the butterfly. We dropped the anchor in downtown Point-a-Pitre which proved to be too busy. The next day we moved back down the channel to anchor off the marina. Learning that the water was free in the marina, we took a slip for three days and did an extensive wash down of our vessel. This was the first time we had used a marina in 1 ½ years, and the cost was only 130 francs ($13.00) per day. I liked these French islands.

On June 2nd, we sailed back to Les Saintes. The Mahogany Shop couple invited us to a local Creole Party. We took them in our Zodiac over to the beach at Sucre where the party was being held in somewhat of a community center. This was where we first heard Souk music that had developed in the French West Indies. The locals were dancing and having a great time. A buffet dinner of couscous and fish ensued. Champagne bottles were held high in the air, and with a swing of a machete they were suddenly opened. Swigs from the bottle were followed by pouring the bubbly into glasses. Whaaaalaaaa! This party certainly had an exotic French flair.

On the 4th, we sailed on down island to Dominica anchoring in Prince Rupert Bay. The guidebook had warned about the boat boys. Some of them were waiting a mile offshore to catch their prey. We did a tour of the Indian River and bartered for a small stock of bananas.

The next day we made it to the southwestern tip of the island anchoring by Scotts Head. We hoisted our anchor early next morning sailing for Martinique. By midday, we had made the northwestern lee of the island where a large number of porpoises greeted us. We later anchored in front of Fort de France to clear into Customs.

We spent two months enjoying the different anchorages in this beautiful lush well organized island. We rented a car and drove to the east side of the island to tour an old historic rum factory. If you ever have tasted Martinique rum, you will certainly remember its peculiar smell. It isn't smooth nor is it pleasant. It is produced in the old traditional way with no modern influence. The aged liqueurs were nice, but I could only drink the regular rum in their famous Ti-punch.

Since we anchored in Anse-Mitan, we visited Trois-Islets nearby. The town has a rich cultural heritage. It was the birthplace of Josephine who married Napoleon Bonaparte and became the Empress of France. A ferryboat ride from Anse-Mitan took us directly downtown of Fort-de-France. It was a large bustling city with many very tall beautiful Creole women.

Our favorite place was to anchor by the beautiful beach of St. Ann on the southeastern coast. A Club Med there provided many more of our notorious adventures. Our group of five sailboats became very talented at sneaking onto the grounds to sample the delights. I told our fellow band of misfits about the problem at the Cub Med in Eleuthera, Bahamas. I advised them not to wear their ratty boating tee shirts and their salt encrusted Topsiders boating shoes.

Dressed as their typical guests, Gentle Member (GM), we would buy the necessary beaded necklaces for drinks to hang around our necks. When one of the security guards would confront us in their broken English, we claimed to be on the red sports team or housed in one of the named cabins such as Campeche which always seemed to work.

We all attended the first evening show after dinner put on by the Cub Med personnel. I surprised everyone in our group by slipping out of my seat. As the stage curtain was raised to reveal the Club Med people, Gentle Organizers (GOs), lined up on elevated rows, they started to sing their traditional song to welcome the newly arrived weekly guests.

I saw one of the GM out in the audience that had sat with us during dinner. She suddenly elbowed my wife who was sitting beside her. She pointed and exclaimed, "Isn't that your husband up on the top row!" While trying to keep up with the GO's singing, I saw the shock suddenly revealed in her face. Soon all our band of naughty sailors had open mouths and wide eyes.

Even some of the Club Med people next to me asked if I had just been assigned to this Club since they did not recognize me. I quickly told them I had just arrived the previous day and kept on singing. I had told Millie I was going to watch the show from the back of the room near the bar. I had quickly formulated this plan after dinner probably because of the two carafes of complimentary wine seduced me into being "baaaaaad", as we say in the islands.

Two weeks anchored by the Club Med provided many entertaining stories. One time after viewing the sights at the nude beach, a group of us ended up in the large spa tub. Two recently arrived couples jumped in beside our devious group. Later, they asked why we were all so tan. We told them we were Club Med groupies that just went from one club to another around the world. The cute little thing sitting beside me asked what I did in the states. I responded that I was in the movie business. I then asked her if she was familiar with the TV show *Dallas*. She replied excitedly that she watched it all the time. I asked her had she seen the episode where South Fork burned to the ground. She replied that yes she had. I responded that I was the Fire Captain trying to save the house. The new GMs were impressed with us. We started calling our pirating band "The Club Med Rejects."

Another one of our devilish deeds was done while our band of brothers was on the public beach adjacent to the Club Med. We were celebrating a marriage anniversary and a birthday. Since it was a double "DO", we started early and were having a great time. We happened to notice a preppie couple walking down the beach towards us from Club Med. Since we knew it was the weekly change over for new guests, we thought we would induct them properly.

I asked if they would take a group photo as they walked by our group. As they got all set to shoot the scene, I gave the prearranged command for the females to drop their tops. They were so impressed that they spent the rest of the afternoon learning how to *Party Hearty*.

On August 8th, exhausted from all of our devilish deeds, our brotherhood of sailors sailed for St. Lucia. We anchored in Rodney Bay and enjoyed all the restaurants located there. A bus trip into Castries provided us with a view of the local island markets. We then sailed down to the small and beautiful harbor of Marigot.

We were starting to understand the boating guide's description of sailing the lee of the Windward Islands. These islands are so tall that the winds wrap around the islands on both ends giving you large confused seas. As you get behind the island, the mountain's contours had rivers of swiftly moving air over the top flowing down into the guts and valleys. You would be gliding along on smooth water and notice ripples approaching your boat. Suddenly, you will get a blast of wind that would heel the boat over without any wave action. You learn to look for these situations before they happen so you won't be caught with your pants down.

Two days later we had a peaceful trip to Bequia. We were now moving fast down the island chain due to being hurricane season. We sailed to Tyrell Bay on the island of Carriacou anchoring for two days. The next passage was an uneventful sail over to the active underwater volcano named "Kick'em Jenny" on our way to Grenada.

As we approached St. Georges Harbor, we could see that the annual Carnival Parade was tramping down the waterfront street with its loud music blaring. We spent four fun-filled days in the harbor replenishing our supplies and seeing the area. It was certainly a most majestic island with its lush high mountains and its spice industry.

Several heartwarming things occurred as we were traveling around. We noticed graffiti painted on the walls of the old buildings that praised the Americans. It had only been two years since the U.S. Intervention that threw out the Cubans. The island was beginning to recover from that repressive regime. Locals would start hugging and thanking us after finding out we were from the United States.

We moved over to Prickly Bay and Hog Island on the south coast. Lots of cruisers were hanging out in this peaceful area. We took a local island bus back to St. Georges on August 23rd to apply for our Venezuelan visas at their embassy. We have taken many of the local buses throughout the island chain. All were very similar with a tiny Japanese minibus filled to overflowing capacity full of colorful locals. It seemed to be a carnival with blaring music, loud conversations, chickens in cages and mothers nursing their babies.

On the 29th, we took the boat back to St. Georges in order to pick up our visas and prepare for the overnight sail for Venezuela.

7

THE GREAT ADVENTURE – YEAR IV

An hour after sunset on 2nd of September 1985, we set our overnight course for Los Testigos which was a small island 80 nautical miles to the southwest. We had to motor until a couple of hours past midnight. We were then able to sail the rest of the way when a good breeze arrived. We spent three days resting and enjoying the white pristine beaches of this tiny island.

Our next sail was 50 miles to Isla Margarita off the north coast of Venezuela which was a popular tourist area for Latin America. After checking into Customs on the 8th in Pampatar, we quickly moved to Polamar for a better anchorage. We fell in with a group of cruisers and found our way around the town. Everything was very inexpensive.

You and your mate could have a fine steak dinner with drinks for less than ten dollars total thanks to the exchange rate. The grocery store prices were unbelievably cheap. They had major brands, but most were made in Venezuela. The Latin culture was a nice change from the previous islands. The locals were very helpful and friendly to this new influx of tourists in cruising boats. After eleven days enjoying Margarita, we sailed for Mochima National Park on the mainland. It is a well protected bay with a small town at its far end. We reunited with two other cruising boats. Our paths had crossed many times in the three years. These reunions were one of the great joys of the cruising lifestyle. Our small group spent two days exploring the bay, snorkeling and consuming lots of the inexpensive Venezuelan beer and rum. After a short but busy reunion, we sailed to the island of Chimana Grande to spend two days recovering all by ourselves.

Our next big port of call was the area of Puerto La Cruz which was a big well protected bay with a large number of cruising boats. This wonderful place had everything a cruiser needed. There were boat yards, marinas, an airport, modern grocery stores, entertainment at the various tourist hotels and great people.

I must add here that Venezuela was very safe and hospitable at this time. The country had only been opened up to boaters for a few years. The country was still stable and its economy was functioning.

While at El Morro Marina for a few days to get diesel and water, we met a very friendly Venezuelan, Freddie Brandt, living on his houseboat *Nav Nav*. He was amazed at the vocabulary of Captain Hook our parrot. Everyone knew Freddie, and we discovered later that he had been a famous soccer ball player.

When he found out that Millie was a belly dancer and had performed throughout the islands, he invited us to a party at his friend's house. He also asked Millie if she would dance to which she readily agreed.

As Freddie drove us up to a very nice home in Puerto La Cruz, we noticed a couple of burly looking men standing around with shotguns. Freddie explained to us that wealthy Venezuelans had security guards for protection. It seems that the Colombians made a thriving ransom business of kidnapping their children. If you didn't pay, they would start sending fingers in the mail to make a point.

The party was a big success although we were sort of shocked when we were introduced to their children. One of the teenage girls had no legs which immediately got our attention. She was very adept at moving around using her arms like legs. Later that night, it was explained that the girl had her legs crushed in a fancy beachside condominium that collapsed during an earthquake. All the children were enthralled with my wife's dancing and constantly escorted her everywhere. This has always been the response to her dances with children throughout her long career.

We had spent over two weeks here in Puerto La Cruz and felt like it was time for a new adventure. So October 10, 1985 just before sunrise, we set sail for Isla La Tortuga to the north. We anchored in the northwest corner next to two other boats. The next day at 3PM we raised the anchor setting an overnight course to Los Roques. The next morning at nine o'clock we arrived at a small cluster of islands similar to the Bahamas. They were very different from the mountainous islands that we had been experiencing during the past year and a half.

These flat islands covered 546 acres and originated from limestone coral reefs. They were a very productive fishery. In 1972, the Venezuelan government declared these islands the Los Roques National Archipelago and started managing their natural resources. The commercial fishing industry had been using the area but was being replaced as a tourist destination for all to enjoy.

We found many of our past cruising friends anchored all around the park during the following days. After enjoying them for a week, we set sail for the mainland to La Guaira which was 80 miles to the south.

We arrived near the Macuto Sheraton on October 19th and anchored in a small anchorage. Millie had planned to fly home to Texas for about three weeks for a long-overdo vacation. She deserved the treat after being on the boat for three years.

I had planned to spend this time hauling, cleaning and painting the bottom of the boat since it had not been done in two years. I had moved my vessel to Club Puerto Azul, a large condominium complex. It had its own marina and boat yard that cruisers could use. The place was amazing in that it had an Olympic swimming pool, bowling alley, cinema, deli and many more amenities that were available. We heard that a year later it was closed to the cruisers after a French boat washed her sails in their gigantic pool. Millie even got to enjoy the place for twelve days after her return in early November.

We even took a side trip by local bus to Caracas. I wanted to buy a new Honda 650 watt generator for backup on the boat. My old 500 watt Honda had finally crashed after four years of hard use in the saltwater environment. While at the Honda dealer, I just happened to mention that were visiting Freddie Brandt in Caracas. The store immediately gave me a ten percent discount. It pays to know famous people.

On November 26th, we started our migration back east leaving Club Puerto Azul at daybreak heading to Carenero. We invited two other boats while anchored there for a big Thanksgiving dinner complete with a baked turkey and trimmings.

Millie, the galley slave, had become quite adept at using the gimbaled stove. She was also growing sprouts and making yogurt from powdered milk. We even had a tortilla press and a supply of masa harina, so we were getting our Tex-Mex treats.

Our next stop was Puerto La Cruz for a couple of days. We headed east again on December 1st for an overnight stay at Mochima. By the 5th, we were back in Isla Margarita to stock up for the passage towards the Mouth of the Dragon which is the body of water between Venezuela and Trinidad. We needed to get as close as we could to be able to make the passage north to Grenada. This easting took four days and three nights. Pargo, Venezuela was where we finally turned north towards Grenada. Our knot meter had logged 852 nautical miles while in this South American country.

Leaving Pargo before sunset, we sailed in big seas, a stiff breeze and a four knot westerly current. We finally made it back to Grenada to a totally different culture. We dropped the anchor in Prickly Bay at ten in the morning for a well deserved rest after sailing all night..

The south shore was full of cruising friends that had crossed our path so many times. It was a lot of fun reminiscing about all the adventures we had experienced together. We spent a lot of time at the Prickly Bay Marina & Restaurant because they now had the satellite television. Most of the cruisers had not seen a live football game since leaving the states. One of our motley crew even had a son playing in a Jet's game which we were able to watch and root for him.

So many of us were hanging around the place that the manager got wind there was a belly dancer among the group. He suggested to Millie that she perform for all the boaters during a Christmas party. It turned out to be a roaring success. I think the manager just wanted to see how professional she was in her performance.

The crux of the problem was that he was planning to have a big New Year's Eve function at the restaurant. He saw a golden opportunity to blow out the competition. He hired Millie for the big party and started advertizing the event featuring a Middle Eastern dancer.

It just so happened there were still a lot of U.S. State Department people in Grenada. They were trying to get the local economy and government running smoothly after the U.S. Intervention in October 1983. After hearing about the unusual entertainment, many of them planned to attend the New Year's celebration at the restaurant.

Like in Antigua, it was such a novelty that he wound up with an enormous crowd with standing room only. After Millie finished her last dance number, several of the State Department people approached her and said they enjoyed her dancing. Some had been stationed in the Middle East and had seen a variety of ethnic dancers. They complimented her professionalism and knowledge of the world's oldest dance.

We moved the boat around to St. Georges on January 7th to stock the boat for our trip up the island chain. Leaving the next day, we motor-sailed past the underwater volcano of Kick'em Jenney only this time it was very different. We were following a large island freighter that started slowly rolling extremely from side to side. We speculated what action we would take if the freighter finally just laid over on it side. After a couple of miles, its movement stabilized to normal much to our relief.

We anchored and checked into St. Vincent & the Grenadines at Union Island. Spending a day exploring the lovely island, we then moved over to Petit St. Vincent to visit the famous P.S.V. Resort. The following day we continued on towards Bequia.

We splashed the hook on the north side of the channel in Bequia's main harbor of Admiralty Bay. The area had been a popular stopping port for boats and was full of cruisers. While there we met one of the homeowners of the famous Moonhole complex.

These unusual homes were started by Tom Johnston in the early sixties and were featured on the front cover of *National Geographic* in the seventies. He started building them in the caves on the southwestern tip of the island out of the natural rocks. As it turned out, most now were on top of the peninsula since the caves proved to be unstable. All were unusual and fantastic. They were done in the "Green" concept long before the world had ever heard of the idea. Some very wealthy families participated in the project. It was a very private and closed community so it was a special treat for us to visit.

On January 16th while still anchored, Millie and I were knocked out of the master stateroom double bunk at two hours past midnight. I was shocked when I slid back the hatch to find the stem of a 146 foot island freighter sticking through my crushed hard dinghy hanging on the davits. I rushed to put on some clothes to survey the damage to my vessel. By the time I returned to the cockpit, the freighter was pulling past me. I noticed it had no steaming lights just some boys running around with flashlights.

My dinghy was crushed to smithereens and my new Honda generator that I stored in it was missing. Our boat's teak tariff rail was cracked in several places, and the wind vane steering system had been damaged.

I noticed a center cockpit boat behind me had not been touched but often wondered what would have happened to it if it had been hit. Someone certainly would have been injured since the aft master stateroom is located there.

I went down below and hailed the freighter that had just struck our sailboat on the VHF radio. After a few anxious seconds, a voice replied. I asked to speak with the captain of the vessel. A reply finally came back stating the captain was in his bunk sleeping. I got the name of the freighter and asked for the captain to meet me in the port's office the next morning. I also asked the person if he had his radar working and why his running lights were not operating. No reply came back from the freighter.

The next morning I found my new generator twenty feet in front of the boat on the sandy bottom. I calculated from collision the boat must have traveled seventy feet before the Honda fell out of the dinghy.

I credit my overbuilt Taiwan hard dinghy hanging in the davits acting as a bumper limiting the damage to the boat. It must have absorbed much of the freighter's momentum. The only big problem now was that we had no dinghy to get to shore. I had sold my Zodiac inflatable in Grenada and had planned to buy a new one in Martinique.

So, this event started our project of how to cruise the islands without a dinghy. I became quite adapt at hollering, "Hey Buddy, can I bum a ride." When that did not work I would go to Plan B by strategically having my longhaired beauty stand on the bow pulpit to do the hailing while I hid below. Plan B always seemed to work!

The next morning we went to the Port Captain's Office to lodge a formal complaint. We found that the captain had a serious drinking problem, and the freighter was half owned by a local family with four sons who were crew. He suggested I formulate an estimate and contact the family.

By the afternoon, I completed the estimates and contacted the family. The mother of the boys was definitely the head of the family as the father was off tending to his goats on the other side of the island. A day later I came back submitting a thirty per cent lower estimate saying I could fix some of the damages. The mother agreed to the settlement within a week. I think she did just to protect her boy's clean record on the freighter.

As it turned out within a week, I was sitting in front of a local bank on the quay telling boaters going in that I would give them a better exchange rate for EC's for their U.S. dollars. I was still trying to exchange some of my settlement of 5,300 EC's in Antigua four months later.

St Lucia was our next sailing stop. Heading up island, we took in the beautiful harbor of Marigot which was considered a hurricane hole even though it is very small. Next, we revisited the bustling harbor of Rodney Bay with its large marine complex and interesting restaurants.

The next island in the chain was Martinique where we spent another round of Club Med fun-filled days near St. Ann on the southeastern tip. Afterwards, we sailed around the south shore of Martinique viewing the historic H.M.S. Diamond Rock. This was a 600-foot pinnacle rock where in 1804 the British Admiralty put 120 sailors with cannons to disrupt Napoleon's French fleet from resupplying the island. We anchored again in Anes Mitan across the bay from Fort de France.

We just happened to have the opportunity to observe Martinique's Carnival during February. It was a wild four day event with street parades coming down to the waterfront from all directions. The first day was a combination of groups singing, drumming bands and cars dragging each other down the streets. Another day we were surprised when she devils and drag queens in risqué costumes paraded through town. The last day of Carnival was Ash Wednesday where all the revelers were covered with ashes. By the end, we were tired and ready to continue our trek up island.

The following day we sailed to St. Pierre to anchor for the night. A volcano in 1902 destroyed the city killing the entire population of 30,000 except for one man being held in the gendarme's dungeon. Even ships in the harbor were damaged or sunk. St. Pierre was considered the Paris of the Caribbean, and the event was a monumental world tragedy at the time.

Sailing to the next island of Dominica, we arrived early in the morning where we were startled by a whale broaching fifty feet from the port stern. It scared me so badly at the helm that I nearly jumped off the boat. Millie was startled awake by the noise as she slept with her head down on the galley table.

We anchored overnight in the large bay of Portsmouth with the Q flag hoisted to the spreaders. Early the next morning, we set sail for Isle Des Saintes, south of Guadeloupe. On February 26th, we met a cruising couple from our days in St. Martin off the main village on Terre Den Haut. We spent a lot of time shopping at the Mahogany Boutique and visiting with the owners.

We sailed on to Guadeloupe to use the marina at Pointe A' Pitre so we could top our tanks and wash the boats with free water. It also made it easier to get off the boat since we were still without a dinghy. We spent the last night anchored just outside the marina with another boat so we could get an early start the next morning for Deshais on the northwestern part of the island.

During the night at about eleven, four young men tried to board our vessel to steal the two outboards hanging from our stern. They were surprised to be met with the loud bang of our hatch sliding open and a big aluminum flashlight illuminating a stainless revolver staring them in the face. The two young men that were boarding our boat immediately fell back into their dinghy. Afterwards, I thought maybe I should have had them swim back to shore and confiscate their dinghy for our use. We sailed into Deshaies by late afternoon of the next day. That anchorage would be our jump off place to Antigua.

On March 3rd, both boats were anchored in English Harbor, Antigua. We visited all our favorite places during the next few days. We had made plans to be in the Virgins by the middle of March to meet friends flying in from Corpus Christi, Texas so we were on a fast track to move. We were able to purchase a new dinghy in St. Barts so our saga of cruising without dinghy was finally over.

Mid-March found us back in the Virgins sailing with our friends from Texas who had managed our mail during the past four years. We were in St. Croix by May entertaining another Texas couple on the boat. While in St. Croix, we discovered that the local SSCA group was having a party in June. The main *Coconut Telegraph* for boaters was the amateur ham radio via the Caribbean Maritime Net so a large turnout resulted. We were able to meet many of our old friends that had crossed our sailing path during the last four years. They even asked Millie to perform the Sultan Dance for an honored guest which was a big hit.

8

HELL, I'M NOT GOING BACK!

We came to realize that we were spending more time in St. Croix which had a large contingent of live aboard cruisers. The harbor in Christiansted was one of nicest that we had experienced. It was easy to get around with the local taxi vans system. There were several big supermarkets and even two shopping centers. There were amenities of the good old states such as fast food chains and telephones that were easy to use. The only drawback we could find was that satellite television was not available from the local TV stations. The football games via video tape were still a week late. This fact made betting on football games with unaware tourist very lucrative.

What we liked best was the friendliness of everyone. The restaurants and the music were fantastic. St. Croix was like a blending of New Orleans and old Key West all wrapped up in a tidy package. It truly became our favorite **Island in the Sun**.

Another perk for making St. Croix our home was the fact that it offered great sailing opportunities. It is an easy day sail to the other Virgins. Sailing to Puerto Rico, St. Thomas, St. John or the BVI provides a wonderful experience just about anytime of the year. It was like having these island adventures right in ones backyard whether it was a four-day weekend or a longer vacation. You could almost hear the Pirates Pub, Foxys or the notorious floating Willy T. beckoning for you to sail over for a mind boggling adventure.

By August of 1986, we found that we were falling in love with the island of St. Croix. Our list of choices at the end of our four year cruising sabbatical was slowly being eclipsed by this realization. One day, it just dawned on the both of us that this was the paradise where we wanted to live. Even some of the cruisers that we had come up island from Venezuela with came to the same conclusion. It just did not make any sense to go back to the States and get back into the rat race. I suppose over the years out on the water and sailing the Caribbean, we had just become **Island People**.

The next big question was how we support ourselves. If you have ever lived in the tropics, it sort of falls out of the sky on what people end up doing to support themselves. I was a dentist but did not want the hassle and the expense of setting up a practice. Another cruiser and I started a reverse osmosis business supplying potable water to businesses.

Millie wanted to open a boutique, but I told her to work in one to see if she really liked it. She promptly got a job at the Buccaneer Hotel's Little Mermaid Shop and loved it during high season. During the off season, she hated the job because it was boring. She later started selling tourist post cards on St. Croix from a supplier in St. Thomas. About a year later, she also started selling island resort wear. She really enjoyed this trade and finally started her own business in September 1989.

She also continued her love for Middle Eastern dancing. She started teaching locals at the Lutheran Parish Hall. Millie had a weekend performances at the St. Croix by the Sea Hotel. Sultan Grams for birthdays and special events were usual weekly gigs. Even the Governor of the Virgin Islands, Roy Schneider, was surprised with a

"Sultan-Gram" during a large banquet at Hotel on the Cay. The event was in honor of ABC's "Good Morning America" Spencer Christian who was on island doing a segment for the show. When Millie pulled out the sword towards the end of her dance, the Governor's security team became extremely nervous. But the show did go on.

The major newspaper of the Virgin Islands, *The Daily News*, started a new section in February 1988 called "Island Life". Millie, aka Serena the Belly Dancer, was featured in the very first one with a full page article with a photo of her dancing by the sugar mill at the Comanche Hotel. A small picture was also displayed on the header of the front page. The article told about how she danced her way through the Caribbean while on a boat and now lives on St. Croix.

The "Daily News" article about Serena, 1988

St. Croix's Middle Eastern population even asked her to perform for a wedding. This was a very traditional event. What was interesting was that she had to dance for the women inside the home before the wedding to gain their approval. Only then was she allowed to dance for the men outside on the back porch. The ladies wanted to make sure she was true to their traditional dance and not some ninety-day wonder.

As the evening progressed, the women asked her to dance for them again. One of the older ladies played Millie's doumbec drum while the rest clapped and voiced their shrill yell. As she left the wedding entourage, the ceremonial gunfire pierced the stillness of the night.

We enjoyed being moored in Christiansted Harbor off Stixx and the Caravelle Hotel from 1986 to 1991. It was like Herman Wouk's novel *Don't Stop the Carnival* atmosphere. I told everyone it was like living on a million dollar piece of property but on a gypsy's budget. One could write a juicy novel on the entire goings on night and day.

Happy Hour usually began on one of the boats. Or maybe, we all would gather at the old Kings Alley Restaurant. Our band of pirates would move the action to the Wreck Bar to listen to Michael Bean's music. After that, we would go to the Moonraker to dance. Our other haunts were the notorious Bilge Bar and the historic Casa Loco. After midnight, we would usually venture to the underground Mews for a late night snack.

Our favorite fancy dining options were the Chart House or the Club Comanche. The Ritz Café or Luncheria's street window was always available for a quick meal. We even had a Burger King and Pizza Hut right in downtown for a fast food fix. Then there was always the

"Roach Coach" or a local Crucian restaurant to sample island food.

A lot of quirky things happened during this time. During another incident in the harbor late at night, I found a naked local clinging to my davits. When confronted, he asked me to call the police because others were trying to kill him. Later, I found out that he had raped a woman living in the nearby housing projects. It seemed that island justice was about to be administrated. Long time knowledge by the locals' claims that anything dumped into Christiansted Harbor is flushed out to sea by all the water washing over its protecting reef.

On the weekends, music blared out into the harbor until four in the morning. You had to turn on a noisy cabin fan to get any sleep if you weren't partying in town. If you were just sitting in the cockpit, you could always watch the honeymooners in the Club Comanche's Sugar Mill chase each other around or some other interesting happenings on the waterfront.

After starting her own business in early September 1989, Millie flew to Orlando on the 14th to attend her first Surf Expo Show. She needed to obtain lines to sell to possible customers. Three days later St. Croix experienced the devastating Hurricane Hugo. Luckily, I managed to be one of 34 boats out of 450 still floating after the storm had passed. We had been on a mooring in Christiansted Harbor since 1986. I took my sailboat to Salt River which was considered to be a safe hurricane hole.

I anchored her with everything I had on the boat. I even spent many hours underwater using scuba gear to tie lines onto a long two inch mooring chain that was buried in the mud. One of my longtime boating friends came by in his dinghy when I had just finished and advised me to get off the boat. The hurricane had not veered away as predicted. It looked like it was going to be a direct hit and had intensified. So, I gathered up some important items, Captain Hook and headed for dry land.

Two other boat owners and I went to a friend's house to ride out the storm. It started blowing several hours later and was unbelievable to witness the intensity continually increasing. The only thing one could hear was the roar of a freight train, the sounds of things blowing apart and loud bangs of various objects hitting something. When the eye went over the island, all of us went outside during this calm to view the damage. Our hearts sank when we looked at the extensive destruction. None of us expected to have anything left resembling a boat.

As the backside of the hurricane started to blow, six people, a dog and a talking parrot huddled inside the washroom making worried plans for the future. Luckily, I had brought some bottles of Cruzan Rum to lessen the painful anguish that everyone was experiencing.

The hurricane had started late Sunday afternoon on September 17th. By Monday morning, we were cleaning up the house while trying to make plans to return to our respective vessels. Most roads were blocked by downed trees and telephone poles. We finally managed to get back to Salt River by noon. My boat had some cosmetic damaged, but the other two were complete losses.

I settled back into the boat and surveyed the damage. I also realized that I had water, food and a good supply of cold beer. I considered myself extremely lucky again to behold the power of the wind and survive. Next, on my agenda was to get word to Millie because St. Croix was cut off from the rest of the world. Amateur radios used by locals and cruisers were the only communication available for the next four days of chaos.

And my message to the outside world that night while sitting next to my ham radio onboard was:

"The boat is OK, Captain Hook is OK & I'm OK."

"And please get a message to Millie Johnson at the Surf Expo Show in Orlando to go to Corpus Christi, Texas and await instructions."

I was able to mail a letter to her about a week later after moving the boat from Salt River to Christiansted. I described all the destruction on the island and said its future looks dismal. I also told her to look for a dental practice for me in the Corpus Christi area since our plans here were blown to Hell.

Since the town's harbor was closed because of a major oil spill, I spent the night anchored at Buck Island. After supper and a few rum drinks, I was sitting in the cockpit listening to Jimmy Buffett. As a big full moon came up over the eastern end of St. Croix, the island appeared to light up just as Jimmy's song "Island" started to play. Tears came to my eyes as the song released its magical words. I spoke out into the night, "My God, I can't go back! I love this Island too much!" Another letter soon followed. I wrote her to forget the dental practice and get your butt back to St. Croix, ASAP!

Oh, there were planes flying onto the island in four days, but they were the 82nd Airborne and relief supplies. Also, the military started to evacuate anyone who wanted to leave on their return flights. The population suddenly dwindled with all the people scrambling to get off island. It was utter chaos with looting and no police.

One day the island was lush, green and vibrant. Following the hurricane there was not a leaf on any of the surviving trees. Within four days, the island smelled like mildew from all the rotting vegetation. It was a mess. There was no electrical power and no drinking water.

Ninety percent of the buildings had roof damage, and half of those also had collapsed walls. Ninety five percent of the electrical poles were down and had to be replaced. It took four months to get the electrical grid up and running. Almost everything had to be reconstructed on the island. Supplies had to be assembled on the mainland almost thirteen hundred miles away. Everything had to be flown or shipped which made it a logistic nightmare.

The military brought in big generators and reverse osmosis units to make potable water for human consumption. St. Croix became dotted with large plastic water buffalos for people to fill their containers. There were military police patrolling the island, and a dusk to dawn curfew was enforced.

"Thank God we were under the U. S. Flag"

The 82nd Airborne stayed until December when they suddenly packed up and disappeared. Later, we found out it was due to the Panama Operation and their participation.

In the middle of October, Millie was able to fly back to St. Croix. She was overwhelmed at the damage. I had moved the boat out to the St. Croix Yacht Club on the east end of the north shore. Only four boats were using their facilities because all the others were either sunk or on the beach.

Our old mooring downtown was off limits after the power plant's fuel tanks had collapsed. The harbor was coated with heavy thick oil, and a major cleanup was underway. There were wrecked and sunk boats all over the place.

During the next six months, we probably spent more time in St. Thomas, St. John and the BVI because those islands still had a viable economy. Millie had obtained several clothing lines to sell. We started making cold calls on potential customers going ashore by dinghy with a duffle bag of samples.

Our best product was an updated crinkly version of the old nylon gym shorts. It was sort of unique at the time in that they folded up into its own pocket. She called them Hurricane Hugo shorts. You could wear them, take a shower in them, sleep in them and travel with them --- a complete island wardrobe! The only other possible thing one needed was some good music and Cruzan Rum.

Millie's business, Serena's, started to take off. We started showing her customers on the boat either at a marina or an anchorage. The island clients loved the ambiance of coming to the boat and being entertained by Captain Hook while seeing her lines. She moved three times to larger spaces in Green Cay Marina over the years from 1989 to 1997. By 1991, we moved the boat into the marina. Her lines expanded to resort wear, sandals, bathing suits, towels and of course more tee shirts. Her biggest line was the original Jimmy Buffett Clothing Company which later became Caribbean Soul.

Millie had sample sales at the store to get rid of the items that were discontinued. She would place flyers at the Marina Office and in all their bathrooms. After the first sale, the *Coconut Telegraph* would spread the word like wildfire.

I would set up outside with a boom box playing Jimmy Buffett music and offer complimentary drinks just to get the customers in the mood. It was hilarious to witness the mad scramble for bargains. Women ran around the office with just panties and bras feverishly trying on things. Sometimes an argument developed when two women would grab the same garment simultaneously. This yearly event certainly brought out the animal instincts of the island ladies.

A few years later it became necessary for her to fly to the various islands and set up in a hotel room to see customers by appointment. I told everyone that it was the perfect job for her!

****She Flies****She Talks****Room Service****

Her business is still thriving today even in these chaotic times. She travels to the islands to show customers and to the states for trade shows. The fax machine has been replaced by emails. Her Blackberry is her constant companion. Four years ago she did not know anything about a computer. Now, everything is done on her laptop. Technology is constantly changing the way she does business. It will be interesting to see what the next ten years will bring to the table.

After my water business dried up in 1992, I even got into the wholesale rag business. I started selling pirate clothes patterned like the flour sack stuff from Mexico and Jamaica. Pirate tee shirts, flags, mugs and other novelty items soon followed. My proudest achievement was marketing Jimmy Buffett music cassettes which were a hit with all the charter boat people.

Modeling Pirate Togs at Serena's Showroom at Green Cay Marina, circa 1993

While on a trip to the BVI in the early nineties, we anchored just off Saba Rock in North Sound, Virgin Gorda. We were getting ready to go up to the Bitter End Yacht Club for dinner when we decided to go for Happy Hour at the newly opened Pirates Pub Bar. Bert Kilbride's latest wife Gayla had converted his old dive boat dock building into a thriving pub business.

Bert has had a colorful life that included being a building contractor and avid spear fisherman on St. Croix in the late fifties. Later, he developed two barren islands in the BVI and was a treasure seeker for 5 decades. In 1967, Queen Elizabeth bestowed the title "Keeper of the Wrecks" upon Bert. His dive business in North Sound was one of the first in the BVI. He also developed the first resort dive course for the industry.

I was wearing the latest design of my pirate pants and hooded shirt. When Gala saw them she wanted them to sell in the Pirates Pub. When I mentioned I had a bunch on the boat, she insisted that I go get them right then. She bought them all and placed an order for more of these wild and crazy outfits.

Sitting around talking to her and Bert was always fun. Bert always had a story to tell. His latest was how he was going to salvage the lead coffin of Sir Frances Drake off of Portobelo, Panama. I always wondered if he planned to have it on display in the Pirates Pub along with all the parrots greeting the arriving customers. Now, that scene would certainly make the *Coconut Telegraph* come to life.

The bartender there just happened to see my shackle ear ring, and said he would really like to get his ear pierced. I jumped up and said, "No Problem, Mon! You'll have the deed done tonight if I can drink on the house." He responded by saying, "Carry on, Mate." I promptly went to the boat and retrieved my piercing gun with a supply of golden studs. Needless to say, it was one of those nights to remember!

March 1997 was the fateful year that we swallowed the hook and moved into a house after fifteen years of living on the boat. I tell people that Millie tricked me into this deal. We decided that instead of renting the office in Green Cay Marina that we would buy a house to operate her business.

Captain Tom, Millie and her brother in Pirate Togs at Norman Island, BVI, circa 1996

I also chartered my boat at various times during these years in St. Croix. I had a U.S. Coast Guard 100 Ton License and a great boat for chartering. We did day sails that did not include Buck Island. This offered a change of pace for people who had already done the National Underwater Park. **Pirate Cruises** of 3 to 8 days to the other Virgins rounded out our chartering business.

Captain Hook the parrot always captured our guests' hearts and stole the show. We would put him out in the cockpit after the end of a charter for the guest to enjoy. He would always go through his song and dance routine. Everyone had to have a photo of themselves with our goofy bird. I guess I should have charged a special fee for that service and pocketed the money for boat drinks as any good blow-boat sailor would have done

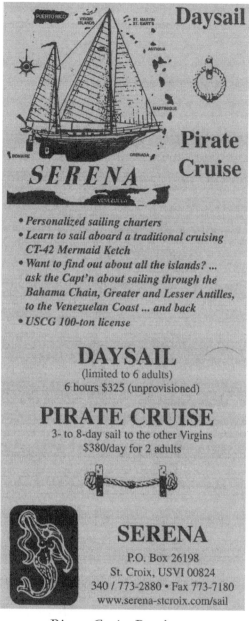
Pirate Cruise Brochure

"Arrrr, Matey! Give me your wine & women!"

The house sits close to two hundred feet up the side of a hill about a quarter of a mile from the north shore.

Our view from the porch overlooks the rainbow of colors of the protecting reef and Buck Island. We named the place "Sailor's Rest". But after living in dirt, fighting all kinds of bugs, cutting bush and the temperature eight degrees higher, I am thinking about changing the name to "Sailor's Purgatory" or better yet "Devil's Rock"!

In 2004, we sold our beloved *s/v Serena*, a CT-42 Mermaid Ketch, after owning her 24 years. I just could not keep up with boat maintenance and the house. The only saving grace about the decision was the view overlooking the Caribbean Sea and the reefs. On a clear day, you can see St. Thomas and at night her lights. Buck Island hides St. John from view, but sometimes you can see the highest peak of Virgin Gorda in the BVI.

View from the porch of our house looking towards St. Thomas

At night, I jump in the cool pool after a soak in the hot tub while looking at the stars. After my shower, I again go out to marvel at the twinkling lights of Christiansted, the loom of the other islands and look at the stars while toweling myself dry. I can almost see us out on those waters **"Sailing the Dream"**.

9

THE CAPTAIN LOOKS BACK

A. Well, was it worth it?

Hell Yes! It was an adventure every day. I would wake up with a cool breeze coming down the hatch while lying in my bunk and thinking that I'm free to do what I want to do or need to do. Or, I could just roll over and look at my beautiful longhaired naked mate lying next to me in my bunk. It would be difficult to beat that kind of a scene.

B. How did you just pack up and leave society?

I had this dream to find that tropical clear water for a very long time. When my responsibilities allowed it and I became financially able, I developed an eight year target date. Luckily, I bailed out two years earlier because by mid 1983 South Texas became an economic disaster due to the oil bust. Also, the office burned up in the summer of 1983. If I had waited, my plans would have been put on hold or maybe would have never happened.

C. Why did you only sail the Eastern Caribbean?

This was my dream. We did think about sailing else where but enjoyed it so much here. We also did not like long passages and cold water. In all of our sailing experiences, the Virgins have been the most enjoyable.

D. Do you regret not practicing dentistry since 1982?

Dentistry was very good to me. I enjoyed a successful practice for 17 years. But after being out in the islands experiencing a whole different lifestyle, I did not want to go back to the rat race. I could not see myself cooped up in a small office paying off a big frigging loan. I found a simpler life fulfilled my needs.

E. Do you miss being in the States?

I can honestly say, "Nope." It was five years, after we sailed from Corpus Christi in '82, before I visited the first time. I'm always anxious to get back to St. Croix when I do go. It is just too damn busy up there.

F. Why St. Croix?

It has one of the most diverse ethnic cultures of any of the Caribbean islands that we have visited. This fact was brought on by several events. The first problem was the extreme poverty that existed in the Caribbean from 1900 to 1960. A mass migration to the States occurred in the U.S. Territories. The Navy making Viequez, Puerto Rico a bombing range in the 1930's brought a large contingent of their Spanish population to St. Croix. The building of Hess Refinery and the Aluminum Plant in the sixties brought many down-islanders. People of Middle Eastern, Indian and Asian origins worked their way up the island chain from Trinidad by the eighties and have added to the mix. Continentals started discovering the island's charm and began moving here as permanent or part time residents. No one ethnic group has control as in the other islands.

Nepotism in the government is prevalent with the indigenous locals. But being a U.S. Territory under the United States Flag and the Constitution added to the mix in what makes this island stand alone above the others.

G. Would you go sailing again?

After living in a house, I tell people that just my wife's shoes would fill up the entire boat. No room for beer and rum! Seriously, I would in a heartbeat, but my body is telling me ---- not so fast big boy. I came to this conclusion when in 2006 I helped a friend sail his 42-foot catamaran back up the island chain from Canouan in the Grenadines to Road Town, BVI. We spent 14 days visiting all the islands that I sailed to in the early eighties. Lots of changes have occurred. A bad back, loss of equilibrium, sun damaged skin and the difficulty of getting upright from being on my knees brings reality into perspective. And I have to add with a bit of humor that boaters do spend a lot of time on their knees. In fact, it has taken six years for the white calluses on my knees to revert back to normal skin. Don't get me wrong, I thoroughly enjoyed the sail. But my body did not like it and convincingly told me.

English Harbor, Antigua: "Moon Raker Six" tied to the quay during the delivery to Road Town, BVI in December 2006

10

The '70s "FIBERGLASS REVOLUTION"

Until 1970, the majority of live-aboard pleasure boats were made of wood which were expensive to buy and to maintain. You had to have big bucks to play the game. There were a few exceptions like the home-built boats such as Piver and Brown trimarans. Rudy Choy and Warram catamarans were also in the mix. By the late sixties, affordable wood sailboats started appearing in the States from Taiwan and China.

The real turning point came when the fiberglass Westsail 32 sailboat appeared on the cover of *Time* magazine in June 1973 with an extensive article. The boat even came in various kit forms for the home builder. The company also sold a sail away version. The cruising sailboat concept was about to become the dream of thousands of people.

An explosion of boat manufacturers followed suit on the west and east coasts. Towns like Costa Mesa and Clearwater became the centers of the fiberglass production sailboat. Names like Irwin, Morgan, Gulfstar, Cal, Catalina and Southern Cross became common in the sailing communities. Even a dentist, Dr.Jack Van Ost, got into the boatbuilding game by building the rugged CSY boats in Tampa for his charter company. Millie and I had the privilege of visiting many of these factories in Tampa and Clearwater area during the late '70s when we were boat hunting.

Designers Carl Alberg, Ted Irwin, Charlie Morgan. William Garden, Thomas Covin, Bill Crealock, Bruce Roberts, Bill Shaw, Thomas Gilmer, Dick Newick and many more became famous in this boat building era. Taiwan builders grew to seventy plus before the 1976 crash that halved their numbers. Boats were being built in barns, dreams were being formulated and sailboats were being outfitted for the cruising dream. It was almost like being in fairyland the excitement was so thick.

Many of these boats built during this rapid expansion of the cruising phenomena are still plying the waters around the world. It just goes to show that most were overbuilt, tough and could take the environment of over forty years of the sea combined with man's abuse.

11

The '80s "CRUISING EXPLOSION"

By 1980, the mass migration to go cruising was in full swing. Thousands of boats had been built, sold and resold. The few cruisers who had ventured out in the sixties and seventies were writing books and magazine articles. "How To" books had complete roadmaps for novices to follow. *Cruising World* was a popular sailboat magazine and clearly the king of the cruising community.

Farmers, factory workers, white collar, young and old were smitten by the thought of going cruising. Even the "Stink Potters" were looking at cruising trawlers as a way to go to sea. East coast snow birds were making the winter trek down the ICW canal to the warmer climates. Georgetown, Bahamas was becoming an annual gathering place for the cruisers.

The average size of the boats was 28 to 42 feet. Most were fiberglass, but others were wood, steel, aluminum or even ferro-cement. The cutter sail plan, the ketch rig and the sloop carried the day over the older schooner, yawl or gaff designed boats. Conversations concerning the best anchor and dinghy were battered around constantly. You could read books and magazines, but learning by doing and making a mistake was the best teacher. Dragging anchors were a constant threat. Everyone was learning the ropes (or lines) of cruising. The Happy Hour would solve most of the heated discussions!

12

The '90s "BIGGER IS BETTER"

The 1990s brought many changes to the cruising community. Boat size increased to 43 to 60 feet. The extra length was needed to haul all the goodies that were being marketed to cruisers. Water makers, generators, air conditioners and washing machines were the new norm. A GPS with chart plotters could give you a constant fix. No more dead reckoning or the SatNav twitch with three plus hours between a fix. Electronics were developing on a fast track due to the Persian Gulf War.

In the eighties, no sailboats went to Trinidad because of its problems. Venezuela had been a favorite cruising ground for years, but they were starting to have crime on cruisers. It was the simple fact that happens in a maturing cruising ground.

A few young Trinidadians had seen the positive economic impact that cruisers had on Venezuela, and they wanted a piece of the action. They developed a yachting center in an old WWII seaplane base called Chaguaramas. Now, it is probably the largest marine service center in the Caribbean.

It was getting crowded out there with all the boats sailing the Caribbean. Marinas were being improved or planned to handle all the traffic. Islands started to see a money cow in the cruisers. Some became greedy and imposed more fees while a few saw the need to accommodate. Boaters always had the option to pick up anchor and sail to another island. Cruisers with their ham radio sets could find out the scoop on where and what happened yesterday all throughout the islands. They could plan for the future to avoid the problem areas.

Hurricanes in the '90s forced most cruisers to go below Grenada, 12 degrees North Latitude, due to their insurance coverage. Most went to Trinidad or Venezuela to haul out and relax. Some stayed around Grenada for the season. It became like an annual trek to hide out.

The upper Eastern Caribbean became sparse with boaters during the hurricane season. Only the bareboat charter companies kept busy by marketing sailing/scuba programs during the summer months to schools, colleges and organizations. The local boaters toughed out the season due to working or not having any insurance of which the boaters called being *Bare-Ass*.

13

Present   "MEGA YACHT MANIA"

All over the Caribbean "Mega Yacht Mania" has become the norm. Whether at existing marinas or completely new facilities, the rush is on to cater to the wealthier boater. The yachts have become so large that Antigua's English Harbor has taken a back seat to Falmouth. The islands of Grenada, Dominican Republic, St. Maarten, St Thomas, St Lucia and Jamaica have all built marinas to cater to these mega yachts. New facilities are being planned in the Turks & Caicos, Anguilla and anywhere the big bucks appear.

Big yachts with enormous paid crews have generated all types of new businesses. It takes a lot of things to keep the mega ship people happy. Marine supply stores, boat yards and outfitters are just the beginning of the list. Hotels, restaurants and casinos are also feeding off them. Even large transport ships have been designed to load them and take the mega yacht any place in the world just for the sake of convenience and money.

It seems that the small cruisers have been left to fend for themselves. Restrictions on the cruisers have been slowly eroding the joy of being out there. The islands have found that mooring fees can generate enormous amounts of cash. Since the middle '90s mooring fields are being put in popular anchorages to the point where it is difficult to find a place to anchor.

If you want to pay for a mooring, you better plan to get there early to find a spot. The BVIs are probably the most notorious offender. Even places like the bay at Marin, Martinique that use to be secluded are now completely filled with charter boat companies and mega yachts. You better get out there soon because all the other islands can smell the money and are planning to install their own money making cash cows.

The islands are trying to limit the small cruisers by imposing all sorts of fees. It has become so expensive in the Bahamas that many boaters are spending less time or avoiding them all together. Cruising fees, harbor fees, park fees, bridge opening fees and increased custom fees are just a few in this endless list. I have to admit that one island was a pleasant surprise in 2006 during my catamaran delivery. Martinique had no fees of any kind to cruise their beautiful island. *Three Cheers for Martinique!*

The small cruisers are still out there plying the oceans. They just have to go farther away from the old cruising grounds or put up with the changes. Maybe, when diesel gets so expensive for the super rich or they all go bust, the age of sail will return to some sense of normalcy like in the old days. Unfortunately, don't count on it to happen in the near future.

My advice for anyone contemplating of going cruising is to follow the words of wisdom from Mark Twain that starts my story! Reread its message to those who dream!

"Twenty years from now you will be more disappointed by the things you didn't do than the ones you did. So throw off those bowlines. Sail away from the safe harbor. Catch the trade winds in your sails. Explore. Dream. Discover."

14

MEMORIES FROM THE LOG

These memories of my **Great Adventure** have been burned into my brain. I can see them so clearly sometimes they bring tears to my eyes while reminiscing or telling a sea story. I feel so fortunate and thankful that I have been able to go to sea with my own boat.

Looking at *s/v Serena's* Logbook and the two small Guest Books has been a pleasure. They helped me reconstruct the timelines of our adventure. The books brought into perspective all the people who have crossed our wake along the way. Not only was it the places, but it also was the people that have made this so great.

We met snowbirds on their various vessels escaping the cold winter months. We saw sailors taking off from the real world. Most were the middle aged ones following their dreams or others just escaping the rat race. Some were young doing it on a dime and having to stop to work to fill the cruising kitty to be able to carry on. Then, there were the truly old retired ones trying their best to fulfill a life long dream. A few had small children who thrived in this environment until around the age of 13. That is when they suddenly wanted to go back to see the shopping malls and participate in being a teenager. We became friends with many of the locals on all these islands that we visited.

Some did the Caribbean in a year, but they had to move often and saw little. While others spent 2 to 3 years taking time to stay and absorb more of the cruising life.

Some became so changed in what they really wanted that they stayed to become island people. We met true adventurers who sailed to other continents. Some even circumnavigated the globe and a few more than once.

I would like to thank all the people over the years that asked, begged and demanded that I put our unusual cruising experiences down on paper so others could enjoy. Well, I finally got off my butt and tried my best. I am not a writer. I'm just telling our story. I hope you enjoy reading these sea adventures as much as I enjoyed living them. Now, I think it is 5 O'clock near St. Somewhere and it is Happy Hour so let's have a toast to the Cruising Life.

Below is a list of all the cruisers that signed our two precious Guest Books. We met many boaters along this journey. These books represent only a small fraction of them. The boaters that are in the Guest Books are the ones we spent days with while exploring new destinations. We partied, had meals and great conversations with them. Kids drew pictures, circumnavigators painstakingly drew their routes around the world and others wrote poems about us. There was a sea of messages placed down on those well worn pages.

Maybe some of you will recognize the boat names. While some will see their boats and realize that in a small way they were part of the process that changed our lives to become--------- **"Island People"**.

GUEST BOOK BOAT LIST

1st Guest Book started in Norfolk, VA at ICW Mile 0 May, '83
2nd Guest Book started at St. Ann, Martinique in June, '85

Date	Boat Name	Information
1983		
May	*Sarah*	32 ft. steel cutter
	World Wind	
	Cherry Bomb/Annapolis	
	Camelot	
	Raven	
June	*Ariki*/South Boston	
Sept	*Kamaaina*	38-foot Cutter
Oct	*Sea Witch*	circumnavigated twice
	Asylum/Mass.	Bristol 40
	Estrellita	Irwin 30
Dec	*Michelle Ann*	S2 36
	Free Bird/Corpus Christi	
	Cinquale	Cape Dory
1984		
Jan	*Windspirit*	Tayana 42
Feb	*White Magic*/Dallas	C&C 37
	Malia/Galveston	Bristol 40
Feb	*Igo*/Canada	Sloop

	Ariel/MD	
	Tortuga/DC	
	Pet Rock/TX	Sampson Ferrocement
	Brenan/TX	
Mar	*Sanctuary*/Sarasota	Chuck Pane 43
	Omoo	DownEast 38
	Sand Dollar	CSY 37 Cutter
May	*Wild Card*	Golden Hind 32
	Tilly Whim/PA	Bowman 36
	Angle Eyes/AR	Morgan OI-41
Jun	*Sea Hawk*	
	Spindrift/CA	Irwin 37 Ketch
Sept	*Rainbow Warrior*	Columbia 26
	Patient Pud/TX	
	Tamaaraa	Tayana 37 Cutter
	Gulf Coast Exit/TX	
Oct	*Rubato*/IN	Shannon 38 Ketch
	Narsook/Canada	
Nov	*Geshwind*/FL	
Dec	*Ramage*/London	
1985		
Jan	*The Better Way*/FL	
	Oriental Lady/WA	
	Eucalpt/Australia	Ketch
Feb	*Black Dragon*	1912 40ft. Cutter
Mar	*Meermaid*/Germany	CT-42 Mermaid Ketch

Mar	*Drummer*/Seattle	39ft. Cutter
	Epeditus/Australia	
	Long Life/Canada	
	Mehitabel/Denmark	
	Golden Dragon	
	HoHoq/Victoria, BC	1938 33ft. Sitzgatten
April	*Terra*/FL	Westsail 32
	Andiamo/New Zealand	
	Aeolus/FL	
	Tarnimara/England	
	Rosemary/Italy	
	Coquina/Quebec	
May	*Wizard*/TX	
	The Moose	
	XOXO	
	Stroma of May/England	
June	*Mardi Gras*/CA	
	Morning Light	Columbia 30
	Tranquility II/VA	Cape Dory
	Mystic/FL	Saber 28
	M'Lady/Pensacola	circumnavigated
	Reverie/FL	
Aug	*Dream Maker*/Boston	DownEast 38
	Paragon/FL	Prairie Cutter 32
Sept	*Perrik*/NCt	
	Nav Nav/Puerto La Cruz	Houseboat

	Dirigo/AZ	Westsail 32
Sept	*God Speed*/NC	57ft. Yawl
Dec	*Xanadu*/St. Croix	Tayana 37
	Oomink/AK	French Aluminum
	Fly Catcher	
	Trew	
1986		
Mar	*Stephanie B*	
June	*Milelower*/CO	Shannon 38
1987		
Mar	*Marijo*/St. Croix	Baba 40
	Moon Lady/FL	CT-41 Ketch
	Tarwathie	42ft Albatross Ketch
July	*Aries II*	46ft Liberty Cutter
1989		
July	*Restless*	Southern Cross 35
1990		
June	*Fidelis*	Tayana 37
	Tigger/Canada circumnavigated	Alberg 37
	Michelle/St. Croix	
	Blackjack/LA	
	Cat Ballou/St. Croix	Nonsuch 30
	Texas Rose/St. Croix	Nautique Motoryacht

** PAGES FROM THE GUEST BOOKS**

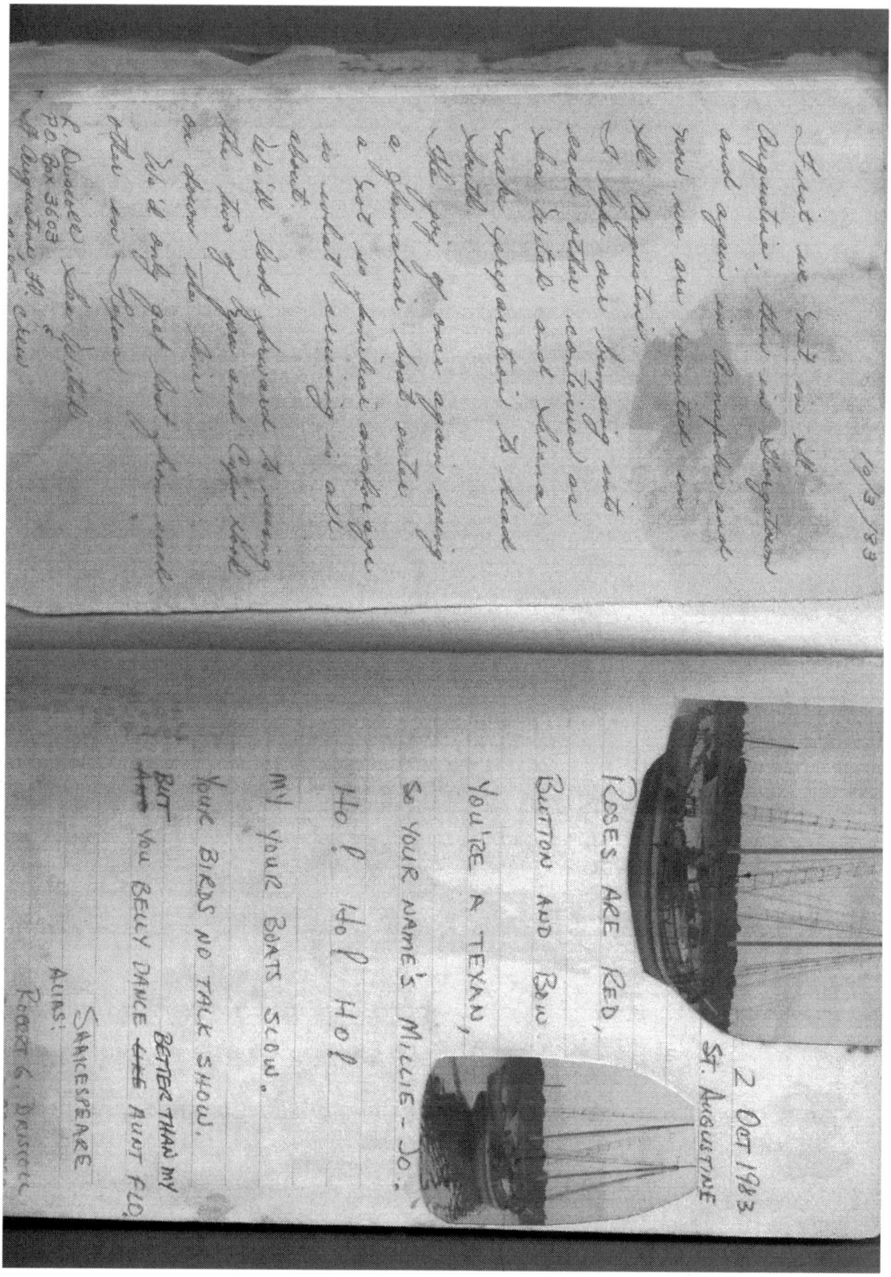
10/3/83
P.O. Box 3603
2 OCT 1983
ST. AUGUSTINE
ROSES ARE RED,
BUTTON AND BOW
YOU'RE A TEXAN,
SO YOUR NAME'S MILLIE - JO.
HO! HO! HO!
MY YOUR BOATS SLOW.
YOUR BIRDS NO TALK SHOW.
BUT YOU BELLY DANCE BETTER THAN MY AUNT FLO.
SHAKESPEARE
ALIAS:
ROBERT G. DRISCOLL

14 Oct 83
Fort Gatlin Fl

Nellie & Tom,

Trouble free sailing!

Kate Wendt Brown
'Asylum'
(40' Sparkman Sloop)
P.O.B. 317
Carver, Mass 02330

The Second Stay: Synopsis

Chapter One: Fighting his way out of the clutches of Fool Klaus, knowing intact Serena reaches the home of Simon von Lessen, a well-known hotel keeper.

Chapter Two: Recalling her peril, Serena appeals to the Vatican, consults the Signor of the Red Zodiac & calls on the Pope

Chapter Three: During the Palace Audience it becomes clear Mr Nixa has kept his Malta & the Pope talks as much as she does.

Chapter Four: Serena waits while Nixa brings back the Petal Puzzle. If she refuses to she is saved. See p.336

Chapter Five: (40) @4
sleeping perspective. To be continued when the knight is saved...

club ORIENT

Ava and Gregory
From the Aussie ketch Eucalypt
who is restocking in Orient Bay
seriously. See you at Club Orient
See you in Asia in Australia
P.O. Box 49 Broadwater USJ
2972 Australia.

Ana Lucia Alves Barbosa
Rua Vicente Gomes ~39
Santana. São Paulo
Brasil

Thank for everything
Lots of Love
Ana Lucia

ORIENT BAY
FEB 1985

Tom & Millie

This Book is a fine idea,
Keeping memories of so many
Friends always fresh.
Enjoyed the sloppy Joe's with
Raisins and our visit aboard
"Serena" Looking forward
to many more good times with you
as we cruise on down island.
Bill & Fay Goodloe

ADDRESS
1915 Beach Ave
Atlantic Beach
FLA 32233

"Black
Dragon"
40' Cutter
6'-3" Draft
Built 1912
in England

Oriental Lady   Sue + John

Sue + John @ Work - Sandy Carithers?

Simpson Lagoon
French St Martin
Jan. 85

Dear Tom + Millie + Capt Hook -
It's been a fun few months
with y'all cousin round about
these parts. Really cheers up a
couple old workin' folks like us!
(Abe changes my vacaberary
(as Tom would say) - I admit I used to
talk with a Texan drawl.) Ever
since Tom told me all about my teeth
at the post-hurricane party at Pablo's
I knew we had some fun folks
around. We'll never forget that
great B-day party @ Pablo's
Pablo's dancing & Sorry you're
leaving soon - but you may just
find us here (still) in a few
months. In any case, I hope
we meet up again somewhere,
sometime. Meanwhile Toten Ahoti
hugs Simulay " Love, Sue + Tom
"Oriental
Lady"

PS My address: S+J Hacking
Box 1467
Oak Harbor WA
98277 USA
(360-675-8851)

Hey you guys,
To a long way from — but there I
and we finally met & I'm glad
See you soon?

Bruce & Fe

English Harbor
April 6, 1985

Heidi Barbara...

Time spent with you has been
delightful but much too short ☺
Hope to meet with you again
sometime —— somewhere ——
Barbara & Bruce

☎ Box 95 3102
Stuart FL 33495

'HOHOO'

S/V HOHOO
HOHOO VIC. B.C.

S.S.C.1

After meeting Easter Monday, Aphigia
with "Serena" & "Yellow SSC1" on a short visit
— turned into a fun afternoon & early evening
— Beautiful English Harbour. Held ola
— Ella dance + seductive music + Bills
"Hooke had a beer up on our 2 terrain. Bell
— when they decided to join the party + win
from Hohoq. I guess they heard him call
here, they didn't! We all hope to meet aga—
+ share time experiences

Ted + Jen de Villa,
4104 Beverley St.,
Victoria Rock. B.C.

33 Lt Springgate
Built 1938 in
Denmark, fished
on Oak. Coast, arrived
Victoria my 1 her/own
4107 Beverel

left Vancouver B.C.
June 1982 on circum
navigation thru —
Red Sea, Med (1yr)
Canaries via
madeira, Atlantic
crossing to barbados
canada + antigua
Nov 2084 — Dec 1985

June 30, 1985
at Annie's

Hope to enjoy many
more with you down —
there in the future.
Thanks for all the good
laughs and information
you've attained —
That Capt Nook sure did
stir my heart and spoil
me rotten! What a meal!
meals, man!
You winds and follow-
ing seas. Be sure to look
us up if you come through
Pensacola again and we'll
have you most guest
of ours

you find us,
Bad & Marylynn
Gatterdam
% Jim & Audrey Daigle
3021 Morningside Dr.
Pensacola, FLA 32503
(904) 433-7879

Tom (alias Pirate) Phillis (alias Belle Somers)
and to Captain Nook the most famous
your gallant galley

It was nice to have met Lady it is
St Anne's and meet up with the
on a wonderful group we all
enjoyed the good times within and

M'LADY
1981-1985

NORTH AMERICA   Pensacola
PACIFIC   MARTINIQUE
                 SOUTH AMERICA
AFRICA   ASIA
0   OCEAN
30
INDIAN   AUSTRALIA
OCEAN   NEW ZEALAND

Date [logo] **Sly PERRIK**

GRENADA .....

Tom & Millie ~

It was terrific to finally get together
_e feel as if we've known you all a long time
he music is greatly appreciated and I shall
_ to sleep nitely with Mr. Buffett in my ear.
_e wish you a great Sail to Venezuela and
_m sure we'll see you soon.

Lots of Luck
Walter & Diana
SCHMIDT/MILLS
c/o GASKINS
111 Brookview Dr.
Jacksonville, N.C.
28540

1 SEPT 85

Date to: Tom, Millie (Serena) and
crew. Hook, Wow... what a Trio !!-
Lucky for me I was at that Fuel
Pump that day we met. - Not every
day one has the Fortune of meetin people
like "you all" and a bird like Capt Hook
No sireeee !!!! Thanks for all the
good times and the Water pick etc.!!
Wish you the best and hope to see you
Again in a short time. - Love
Fuckly Brandt

Pto La Cruz
Marina El Morro
Lecherias, Edo. Anzoategui
6/10/85

life is only born just to
die. "School" because I'm
going   see ... ____
the gist ev'ry friday noon

Folks, Times Per Such a Beautiful
Time. Slong gone Lives & Good
Times will are. I'm Happy -
Looking forward To More.
Love Ya - Gavin
Gavin,
"Brey Berk cowboy!"
"Dude on"

Date 8-26-86

To: Millie, Tom, & Capt. Hook

A Song of my Love for A Boat
            by Serena 22

THUMBIN' BOATS ON A SUMMER DAY
HITCHED A RIDE TO AN ISLAND PLACE
I FELL IN LOVE WHEN I SAW HER FACE
AND SOMEONE TOLD ME HER NAME
A TRAVEL BABY - A TRUDI GIRL
NOW A WOMAN ON THE WORLD
I KNEW THE MOMENT THAT I CLIMBED ABOARD
I'D NEVER BE THE SAME

. OH SERENA
YOU'RE MY SWEET SERENITY
NO ONE ELSE COMES BETWEEN YA
EVEN WHEN WE'RE APART

- OH SERENA
IN MY DREAMS I HAVE SEEN YA
SLOWLY LEAVE THE MARINA
AND SAIL AWAY WITH MY HEART

Date

LIKE A TALE FROM A Story Book
SINGIN' BIRD - CAPTAIN Hook
CAPTAIN CRUNCH IS ALL IT TOOK
- WE WERE ON OUR WAY
SHE LET ME RIDE UPON HER BOW
LIFE WAS EASY, SHE SHOWED ME HOW
I ONLY WISH I KNEW WHERE SHE NOW
I KNEW WHAT I WOULD SAY -

OH SERENA
YOU'RE MY SWEET SERENITY
NO ONE ELSE COMES BETWEEN YA
EVEN WHEN WE'RE APART
- OH SERENA
IN MY DREAMS I HAVE SEEN YA
SLOWLY LEAVE THE MARINA
AND SAIL AWAY WITH MY HEART

        BRING BACK...

SERENITY OL BOAT
SAILING FROM COSTA SIX TO BACK 15

Date April 16 - 24, 1988   St. Croix to
                                 B V I 's
                                 Cruise

Millie + Tom —
We will always remember these 9 days
the will always remember to + running to
about "Cock a doodle" to
BVI's with you and Captain Bob. We
could use these could that experience
of seeing + doing all that we did with anyone
else. You carefully planned + gave us
everything from sights + sound + watching +
waiting + your concern for our floating
on land + your concern for our floating
a happy trip. And that it was! Having
that Cguinbar with 2 friends made the
cruise just that much more. We'll remember
Captain Bob's "performance" on "very Off" mornings
You and "Millie's smile." Even if you resembled
Luke's snoring + the silence (lovely) since —
too" on the tray. Having My more happy
memory days. Thanks + Love! Angela +
                          Mike + Carol sr.

Date June 24, 1990 Christiansted, St Croix

You'll always be able to reach us by the lamp in your heart

TIGGER

Date

Dear Tom, Millie &

It took awhile, but when we finally got together didn't it make a party!!! We have nothing original to say. Someone has already said it all. However, let us add our praises for the "sweetest little ole' Texans to come down the pike. You're fine folks (& bird) and it's real nice to call you friends.

Our livers might start complaining but it'll take more than Texans & #@ poi-don Canucks ~ you gave it a good try tho' Tom. Your cheeks - were delicious Millie. & Cap'n Hook, you're a sweetheart. You can count on my heart anytime. Thanks for a beautiful time.

Love to Y'all.
Ron & Ei. ☺

The smartest bird we've ever met.
He made us pay too Popeye!

Ron & Eileen Holmes aboard Tigger A31 % L. McCormick 861 Hamilton Rd. P.O. Box 683 Clearwater, Ontario Canada N0J1C0

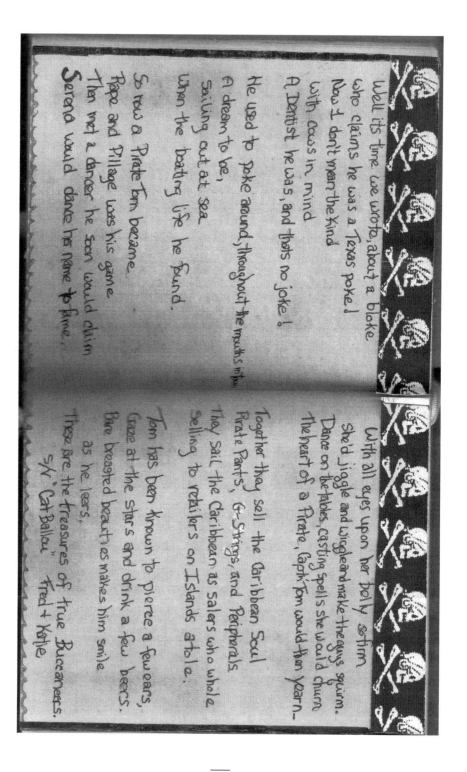

Well it's time we wrote, about a bloke
who claims he was a Texas poke!
Now I don't mean the kind
with cows in mind
A Dentist he was, and thats no joke!

He used to poke around, throughout the mouths in pain
A dream to be,
Sailing out at sea
When the boating life he found.

So now a Pirate Tom became.
Rape and Pillage was his game.
Then met a dancer he soon would claim
Serena would dance her name to fame.

With all eyes upon her belly so firm
She'd jiggle and wiggle and make the guys squirm.
Dance on the tables, casting spells she would churn
The heart of a Pirate, Cap'n Tom would then yearn—

Together they sell the Caribbean Soul
Pirate Pant's, G-Strings, and Peripherals.
They sail the Caribbean as sailers who whole
selling to retailers on Islands atolle.

Tom has been known to pierce a few ears,
Gaze at the stars and drink a few beers.
Bare breasted beauties makes him smile
as he leers,
These are the treasures of true Buccaneeers.
s/v "Cat Ballou" Fred + Katie

144

15

EPILOGUE

Truly, I have been blessed in my life. I have lived my life to the fullest. I am fortunate not to have had many downsides. I have survived hurricanes and incidents with my various boats. I've had adventures that people dream about but are too locked into their life to drop the lines and just sail away. There are dreamers and doers. I thank whatever higher powers there are out there to have had the adventure of a lifetime.

I have two wonderful sons who are successful plying through the seas of life. I tried to make it possible for them to decide their future life's work without pressure from me. I am extremely proud of what they have accomplished. In my life, I did it my way and wanted them to do the same. I believe a self made man builds character and success. I just wish for them to be as happy and content in their lives as I have been in mine. I want them to remember the quote from Mark Twain and better understand why I sailed away to fulfill my dream. They have both visited us over the years while we were cruising and in St. Croix. They have seen places and different cultures that most people never would have the opportunity to see. They have had adventures that others read and dream about but never experience.

"Now, the *Rest of the Story*"   Paul Harvey

I have been fortunate to have found a woman I think would follow me to the far ends of the earth. A lover, soul mate, adventurer and a wife all wrapped up in a petite cute body. She has been a joy to be with from day one. Her personality is always positive and bubbly. She is a self made woman with an interesting past.

When we first started dating she could not even swim. But she knew a life with me included being on the water. On her own she took swimming lessons at the local YWCA. After completing that course, she immediately enrolled in a local dive store's NAUI scuba course. It was comical to see her try so hard to complete the course because she still wasn't a proficient swimmer. In those days, the courses were brutal and very difficult. She received her certification card with sheer determination and hard work.

Millie's Certification Card, 1976

During our next two years of diving, she would ride my tank and constantly look at her pressure gauge just to be on the safe side. Then one day, she must have passed through her comfort zone because she stated to wander off playing with the fish. I decided to buy us both tank bangers just so I could keep her under control while diving.

As a 15 year old, she was put on a Greyhound bus in Stanford, Florida by the FBI and sent back to San

Antonio, Texas to be reunited with her widowed father. She had escaped from abusive adoptive parents who came into her life after her mother died when she was just 9 years old. Millie started working from the age of 16 in a High School Distributive Education Program at Woolworth's and Sears. She had to make her own way in life at an early age.

After graduating from High School in 1963, she worked in a doctor's office and then at the TB Hospital in San Antonio. Later, she landed a job at the San Antonio Chamber of Commerce and was later transferred to the Convention & HemisFair Department for its upcoming grand opening in 1968. She had blossomed into a successful networking person.

During the Vietnam War when her first husband was drafted, she followed him to the Panama Canal Zone. She promptly got a temporary job as a civilian working for the Defense Department. We even have an old photo of her opening the Mia Flores Panama Canal locks.

In Corpus Christi, she was an assistant to the food and beverage manager at the Holiday Emerald Beach Hotel. She later moved to the Sheraton Marina Hotel to become the director of sales servicing conventions. She traveled all over the state presenting her memorable "Sales" speeches.

In 1975, she became the Red Carpet Beach Hotel's sales director because she was now living out on Padre Island. She later started her own company servicing the convention trade in the Corpus Christi area. Then, by default, she landed up in my dental office substituting for employees who didn't show up for work. Millie became a valuable asset to my practice. In fact, I truly believe many of my patients just came in to see her because she was so pleasant and friendly.

Millie has one funny attribute that I must share to make her story complete. She talks so fast that she gets her words all jumbled up. I think the synapses in her brain can not keep up with her talking. We have had many good laughs over the years regarding this peculiar speech pattern.

During the last couple of years, I have been trying to write these misspoken words down when they happen. But I have only obtained a small fraction of them because of "CRS", as we say in the islands. Below is the current collection of these "Gems" and she is probably going to kill me for doing this for posterity.

**** MILLIE-ISMS ***

Word	&	Millie
1. Porno Stars		Promo Stars
2. Werewolf		Weirdwolf
3. Giraffes		Carafs
4. Smoggy		Smuggy
5. Ailments		Elements
6. Scab		Scalp
7. Sheppard's Pie		German Pie
8. Neosporin		Neosperum
9. Parking Lot		Porking Lot
10. Vulnerable		Varneble
11. Alumni		Aloomni

12. Outback	Outhouse
13. Planter's	Patter's
14. Osteoporosis	Osmosis
15. Urn	Yurn
16. Cat Scan	Scat Can
17. Add Water	Liquidfy
18. Cremated	Premated
19. Grammy Awards	Granny Awards
20. Regiment	Regitament
21. Euros	Arrows
22. Truncated	Turnicated
23. Tsunami	Pasamii
24. Heimlich Maneuver	Heineken M.
25. Reconciliation	Reconsolidation
26. Prenuptial	Preniptial
27. Perks	Quirks
28. Eco	Echo
29. Indescribable	Indisscrbly
30. Shrivels Up	Swivels Up

Blowing of the Conch Horn
Signals
* *The End of Our Story* *

(Contact Rob for Details)